MOTHER TERESA

MODERN SPIRITUAL MASTERS
Robert Ellsberg, Series Editor

This series introduces the writing and vision of some of the great spiritual masters of the twentieth century. Along with selections from their writings, each volume includes a comprehensive introduction, presenting the author's life and writings in context and drawing attention to points of special relevance to contemporary spirituality.

Some of these authors found a wide audience in their lifetimes. In other cases recognition has come long after their deaths. Some are rooted in long-established traditions of spirituality. Others charted new, untested paths. In each case, however, the authors in this series have engaged in a spiritual journey shaped by the influences and concerns of our age. Such concerns include the challenges of modern science, religious pluralism, secularism, and the quest for social justice.

At the dawn of a new millennium this series commends these modern spiritual masters, along with the saints and witnesses of previous centuries, as guides and companions to a new generation of seekers.

Already published:
Dietrich Bonhoeffer (edited by Robert Coles)
Simone Weil (edited by Eric O. Springsted)
Henri Nouwen (edited by Robert A. Jonas)
Pierre Teilhard de Chardin (edited by Ursula King)
Anthony de Mello (edited by William Dych, S.J.)
Charles de Foucauld (edited by Robert Ellsberg)
Oscar Romero (by Marie Dennis, Rennie Golden,
    and Scott Wright)
Eberhard Arnold (edited by Johann Christoph Arnold)
Thomas Merton (edited by Christine M. Bochen)
Thich Nhat Hahn (edited by Robert Ellsberg)

Forthcoming volumes include:
Flannery O'Connor
Edith Stein
G. K. Chesterton

MODERN SPIRITUAL MASTERS SERIES

MOTHER TERESA

Essential Writings

✝

Selected
with an Introduction by
JEAN MAALOUF

ORBIS BOOKS

Maryknoll, New York 10545

SL
TER

Founded in 1970, Orbis Books endeavors to publish works that enlighten the mind, nourish the spirit, and challenge the conscience. The publishing arm of the Maryknoll Fathers and Brothers, Orbis seeks to explore the global dimensions of the Christian faith and mission, to invite dialogue with diverse cultures and religious traditions, and to serve the cause of reconciliation and peace. The books published reflect the views of their authors and do not represent the official position of the Society. To learn more about Maryknoll and Orbis Books, please visit our website at www.maryknoll.com.

Manufactured in the United States of America

Library of Congress Cataloging-in-Publication Data
Teresa, Mother, 1910-
  [Selections. English. 2001]
  Mother Teresa : essential writings / selected with an introduction by
Jean Maalouf.
    p. cm. – (Modern spiritual masters series)
  ISBN 1-57075-379-2 (pbk.)
    1. Meditations. I. Maalouf, Jean. II. Title. III. Series.
BX2182.3 .T4713 2001
248.4'82 – dc21
                                                    2001032897

Contents

6

Sources

APMT   Eileen Egan, *At Prayer with Mother Teresa,* comp. and ed. Judy Bauer (Liguori, Mo.: Liguori Publications, 1999).

GG   Mother Teresa of Calcutta, *A Gift for God: Prayers and Meditations* (New York: Harper & Row, Publishers, 1975).

HJ   Mother Teresa, *Heart of Joy: The Transforming Power of Self-Giving,* ed. José Luis González-Balado (Ann Arbor, Mich.: Servant Books, 1987).

HW   Mother Teresa, *In the Heart of the World: Thoughts, Stories, and Prayers,* ed. Becky Benenate (Novato, Calif.: New World Library, 1997).

JWS   Mother Teresa, *Jesus, the Word to Be Spoken: Prayers and Meditations for Every Day of the Year,* comp. Brother Angelo Devananda (Ann Arbor, Mich.: Servant Books, 1986).

LJ   Mother Teresa, *Loving Jesus,* ed. José Luis González-Balado (Ann Arbor, Mich.: Servant Publications, 1991).

LS   Mother Teresa of Calcutta, *Life in the Spirit: Reflections, Meditations, Prayers,* ed. Kathryn Sprink (San Francisco: Harper & Row, 1983).

MLP   Mother Teresa of Calcutta, *My Life for the Poor,* ed. José Luis González-Balado and Janet N. Playfoot (New York: Ballantine Books, 1987).

MT   José Luis González-Balado, *Mother Teresa: Her Life,
        Her Work, Her Message, a Memoir* (Liguori, Mo.:
        Liguori Publications, 1997).

MTB   Navin Chawla, *Mother Teresa: The Authorized
        Biography* (Boston: Element, 1992).

MTLL   Lush Gjergji, *Mother Teresa: To Live, to Love, to
        Witness — Her Spiritual Way,* trans. Jordan Aumann,
        O.P. (Hyde Park, N.Y.: New City Press, 1995).

MTLW   Lush Gjergji, *Mother Teresa: Her Life, Her Works*
        (Hyde Park, N.Y.: New City Press, 1991).

MTR   *The Mother Teresa Reader: A Life for God,*
        comp. LaVonne Neff (Ann Arbor, Mich.: Servant
        Publications, 1995).

MTWL   Edward Le Joly, S.J., *Mother Teresa: A Woman in
        Love* (Notre Dame, Ind.: Ave Maria Press, 1993).

OHFL   Mother Teresa, *One Heart Full of Love,* ed. José Luis
        González-Balado (Ann Arbor, Mich.: Servant Books,
        1984).

OW   Mother Teresa, *In My Own Words,* comp. José Luis
        González-Balado (Liguori, Mo.: Liguori Publications,
        1996).

SBG   Mother Teresa of Calcutta with Malcolm Muggeridge,
        Something Beautiful for God, 1971 (Garden City,
        N.Y.: Image Books, Doubleday, 1977).

SP   Mother Teresa, *A Simple Path,* comp. Lucinda Vardey
        (New York: Ballantine Books, 1995).

SVS   Eileen Egan, *Such a Vision of the Street: Mother
        Teresa — The Spirit and the Work* (Garden City, N.Y.:
        Doubleday, 1985).

TS   Mother Teresa, *Total Surrender,* ed. Brother Angelo
        Devananda (Ann Arbor, Mich.: Servant Books, 1985).

WLB   Mother Teresa, *Words to Love By*... (Notre Dame, Ind.: Ave Maria Press, 1983).

WLWP   Mother Teresa of Calcutta and the Missionaries of Charity, *Works of Love Are Works of Peace* (San Francisco: Ignatius Press, 1996).

Acknowledgments

For permission to reprint excerpts from copyrighted material, the publishers gratefully acknowledges the following:

Ave Maria Press, for *Words to Love By...Mother Teresa*, ed. Frank Cunningham, copyright © 1983 by Ave Maria Press, P.O. Box 248, Notre Dame, IN 46556.

HarperCollins Publishers, Inc. for *Mother Teresa of Calcutta: The Authorized Biography* by Kathryn Spink, copyright © 1997 by Kathryn Spink; *Something Beautiful for God: Mother Teresa of Calcutta* by Malcolm Muggeridge, copyright © 1971 by The Mother Teresa Committee; *A Gift for God* by Mother Teresa, copyright © 1975 by Mother Teresa Missionaries of Charity.

Liguori Publications, for *At Prayer with Mother Teresa*, ed. Eileen Egan and Judy Bauer, copyright © 1999; *In My Own Words* by Mother Teresa, ed. José Luis González-Balado, copyright © 1996, Liguori Publications, Liguori, MO 63057, www.liguori.org.

New City Press, for *Mother Teresa: Her Life, Her Works* by Lush Gjergji, © 1991; *Mother Teresa: To Live, to Love, to Witness — Her Spiritual Way* by Lush Gjergji, © 1995.

New World Library, for *In the Heart of the World: Thoughts, Stories & Prayers* by Mother Teresa, ed. Becky Benenate, copyright © 1998 by New World Library, Novato, CA 94949, www.newworldlibrary.com.

Servant Publications, for *Heart of Joy*, © 1987 by José Luis González-Balado; *Jesus, the Word to be Spoken*, © 1998 by Servant Publications; *Loving Jesus*, © 1991 by José Luis González-Balado and Missionaries of Charity; *One Heart Full of Love* by Missionaries of Charity for English Translation, © 1988; *Total Surrender*, © 1985 by Missionaries of Charity. Published by Servant Publications, Box 8617, Ann Arbor, MI 48107.

Introduction

The Image and Beyond

†

By probing and transcending the popular image of Mother Teresa, this book explores the very heart of her spiritual life and vision. Mother Teresa, who called herself "a pencil in the hands of God" (MT, 23), allowed God to use her life to write a living gospel for our time. By letting the light of Christ shine in her life, she became part of "the light of the world" (Matt. 5:14). This is why Father Edward Le Joly, S.J., who knew Mother Teresa from the beginning of the Missionaries of Charity, affirmed that "in the history of Christianity, Mother Teresa has been more than a personality; she has truly proved to be an event" (MTWL, 7).

But who really was this "event," this world phenomenon called Mother Teresa? Who really was the person beyond the image? What was her vision? How and why did she do what she did? Why was she able to touch so many lives? What was the driving force that made her a modern spiritual master?

MOTHER TERESA'S TRUE IDENTITY

The woman who is known as Mother Teresa was born on August 27, 1910, in Skopje, Macedonia (then Albania). Her given

name was Agnes Gonxha Bojaxhiu. She was the youngest of
three children. In 1928, she joined the Loreto order in Dublin,
Ireland. The following year she went to Calcutta, India, to begin
missionary work. There, in 1931, she took her first vows and
became Sister Teresa. Initially she taught at a school of her
order, St. Mary's High School, in Entally, where she later became the principal. In 1937, she took her final vows. She loved
the school, and she was very popular with the girls. It seemed
that everything was going well for her and that she had everything she wanted. But something bothered her and made her
sad. Every time she looked out of her window, beyond the pro-
tecting walls of the convent, her eyes were shocked by the sight
of the worst slums in the world. Then, as she related, "it was on
the tenth of September 1946, in the train that took me to Darjeeling, the hill station in the Himalayas, that I heard the call of
God. In quiet, intimate prayer with our Lord, I heard distinctly,
a call within a call. The message was quite clear: I was to leave
the convent and help the poor while living among them. It was
an order. I knew where I belonged, but I did not know how to
get there" (MLP, 8).

Today the Missionaries of Charity commemorate September 10 as "Inspiration Day." But at the time Sister Teresa did
not regard her insight as a vision or a pseudomystical experience
in a sacred place. She simply knew that God wanted her to do
something different. Her "call within a call" took place on a
slow-moving train traveling from Calcutta to Darjeeling on September 10, 1946. Her inner being knew it, and a passion was born.

Sister Teresa felt that her vocation as a nun was entering a
new phase. She understood that she had to consecrate her life
totally to the poorest of the poor. Consequently she asked permission to leave the enclosure of the convent while remaining
a nun. The permission from her superiors and from Rome was
two years in coming. Finally on August 16, 1948, she replaced
the religious habit of the Sisters of Our Lady of Loreto with a
white sari and set out to fulfill her new mission.

The "second call" was as clear as her first, but also different. Unlike her entry into Loreto, the second call had no established route to follow, no structures, no rules, no motherhouse — nothing. Apart from the call, the new passion, and the determination, everything was unknown. "I knew where I had to go," she said, "but not how to go there" (MT, 61). Later, she said that leaving the Sisters of Loreto was harder than leaving her family and her country.

Now that she was on her own, Sister Teresa's first steps took her to Patna, north of Calcutta. The Medical Mission Sisters, who provide medical service for the poor, helped her to acquire a basic training in medical first aid and nursing care. In the three months she spent there, she also learned the important principles of nutrition and hygiene, and how to give injections, prescribe medicines, and manage a medical facility.

In December 1948, she returned to Calcutta, where she was given hospitality by the Little Sisters of the Poor. From there, she began her work at the Motijhil slum, just a few miles away. Building on her previous experience, she started by gathering children under a tree to offer lessons on the alphabet and personal hygiene. This led her to make contact with her students' families. She visited them in their homes and helped them with cleaning and with whatever they needed. The depth of poverty of this city's destitute was so great that they considered themselves fortunate if they were able to obtain one *rupee* (about eleven cents) a day. Every day their hunger was growing at the same pace as their hopelessness. Sister Teresa did not have money to give them. Instead, she gave of herself, of her energy, and of her time. She offered them what matters most: her love.

Sister Teresa's new calling was very difficult. She experienced bitter moments of exhaustion, anguish, and especially loneliness. The happy days as a Loreto sister certainly came to her mind. But she prayed, "My God, I choose freely to remain faithful to my decision, and to do only your will" (APMT, 63). She felt that her vision was so great that she wanted to overcome every difficulty. She certainly remembered St. Paul, who wrote: "I can do all things through him who strengthens me" (Phil. 4:13), and she lived by this faith.

Soon after, a large donation allowed her to rent two rooms, which she used as schoolrooms and a small medical facility. Then, little by little, more students came to her, more donations were sent, and volunteer teachers appeared. Now she was able to move on to another slum and create another school. Her mission continued to grow.

In 1950, Sister Teresa founded the Order of the Missionaries of Charity and became officially mother superior, or Mother Teresa — a title some people had been using since she had become principal of St. Mary's School in 1937. The decree of recognition of the new congregation confirmed in a prophetic way the wishes of the Missionaries of Charity expressed in these lines:

> To fulfill our mission of compassion and love to the poorest of the poor we go:
>
> - seeking out in towns and villages all over the world even amid squalid surroundings the poorest, the abandoned, the sick, the infirm, the leprosy patients, the dying, the desperate, the lost, the outcasts;
>
> - taking care of them,
>
> - rendering help to them,
>
> - visiting them assiduously,
>
> - living Christ's love for them, and
>
> - awakening their response to his great love. (SVS, 42)

From 1950 to 1959, Mother Teresa worked in establishing official headquarters for her order in Calcutta, where she founded Nirmal Hriday, the first home for the dying. In 1963, the Missionary Brothers of Charity began. Pope Paul VI gave her missionaries official approval in 1965, and they started to expand beyond India. At the present time they are in more than a hundred countries, taking care of the poorest of the poor, the sick, the dying, and children.

Mother Teresa survived her first heart attack in 1983, and a second in 1989. Despite her wish to step down, she was re-elected superior general of her order in 1990. On September 5, 1997, Mother Teresa died at age eighty-seven. There followed an Indian state funeral, the first of its kind, since Gandhi's assassination in 1948, for a person who had not held a public office.

The funeral itself, a three-hour ceremony attended by representatives of national and foreign governments, was partly a Roman Catholic rite and partly a memorial service performed by people of other faiths. Angelo Cardinal Sodano, the Vatican secretary of state who delivered the eulogy on behalf of Pope John Paul II, said: "The entire church thanks you for your luminous example and promises to make it our heritage.... I thank you for all you have done for the poor of the world.... Dear Mother Teresa, rest in peace."[1]

Mother Teresa received worldwide praise in her lifetime as well as many awards, including the Medal of Freedom and the Nobel Peace Prize. All these honors were an important dimension of her public role. But, in fact, they reflected very little of what she really was. All the public acclaim could have spoiled her, but it didn't. Her true self was much deeper. To a journalist who asked her about her own identity, she replied: "By blood and origin, I am Albanian. My citizenship is Indian. I am a Catholic nun. As to my calling, I belong to the whole world. As to my heart, I belong entirely to the heart of Jesus" (SVS, 357).

When a businessman advised Mother Teresa about the necessity of a business card, especially when she had to solicit donations for the poor, she had one made up that said: "Jesus is happy to come with us as the truth to be told, as the life to be lived, as the light to be lit, as the love to be loved, as the joy to be given, as the peace to be spread."[2] This was her true self and her passport to the hearts and souls of countless people. Her identity? "It is no longer I who live, but it is Christ who lives in me" (Gal. 2:20).

Mother Teresa was what she was: a person who stood for her principles and beliefs. She had a special call, rooted in her love of Christ. She loved him in the poorest of the poor. She infused the world with a fresh air of serenity and a sense of the dignity of all human beings as God's children. Mother Teresa challenged people to think differently and to change their conception and way of life. She was driven by a certain vision and followed a particular path in holiness, all with a clarity of purpose that transcended the image the media had created about her.

MOTHER TERESA'S FUNDAMENTAL VISION

According to Sister Brunet, a nun who was with her at the end, Mother Teresa's last words before she died were: "Jesus, I love you. Jesus, I love you."[3] This very love was the story of Mother Teresa's life, and the driving force as well as the justification of all that she had done, "something beautiful for God" (GG, 69).

There was never a doubt about who owned the heart of this nun. She had always been adamant about this: "We are not social workers, we are not nurses, we are not doctors, we are religious.... All we do is for Jesus" (MTWL, 45–46). "All I do is for Jesus. It is Jesus I serve in the poor, it is Jesus I serve twenty-four hours a day" (MTWL, 36).

Where was Mother Teresa's Jesus? He was in the Bible, in the church, in her prayer, in the Eucharist, in her sisters, in the heart of everyone she met, and especially in the poorest of the poor and the lowest of the low. Jesus was in disguise in each one of them. Jesus was behind the foundation of her order. Jesus was behind all that she did.

Malcolm Muggeridge, in his 1971 book *Something Beautiful for God,* wrote that she could "hear in the cry of every abandoned child, even in the tiny squeak of the discarded fetus, the cry of the Bethlehem child; . . . recognize in every leper's stumps the hands which once touched sightless eyes and made them see, rested on distracted heads and made them calm, brought back health to sick flesh and twisted limbs" (SBG, 18). She said, "We do what others don't do" (MTWL, 40).

Mother Teresa's prophetic vision was not found in books and magazines, but in the eyes of the sick, the dying, and the hungry children. She read the signs of the times in the slums of Calcutta, the violent streets of the world, and the loneliness of human hearts everywhere. Every time she saw a need, she did something about it.

People who have such a vision are luminous, transparent, and captivating. They radiate compassion and cheerfulness. One is compelled to be in their company, not necessarily for what they say but for what they are. They are true leaders. Their genuineness is irresistible.

MOTHER TERESA'S LEADERSHIP

Before he sent his disciples to lead the world to God, Jesus told them, "Follow me, and I will make you fish for people" (Matt. 4:19). A true leader, in Christian life, is a true follower — not of people's whims, but of God's will. Mother Teresa was such a follower, and therefore such a leader.

By surrendering totally to God, trusting the divine providence, and just being "a pencil in the hands of God," she was able to bring hope to people, to touch their wounds, and to heal their lives, leading them to the Christ who was present within them.

Mother Teresa was a person of principles. She was straightforward, courageous, uncompromising, bold, and challenging.

She was never afraid to speak her mind before any audience, even if — and perhaps especially if — that audience seemed to disagree with her. She had the capacity to move, inspire, and mobilize people, making a difference in their lives and through them in the lives of others. She exhibited to others new possibilities and new ways for living. She empowered her followers with the strength of Christ so that they could act together in pursuit of a goal. Such were the qualities of leadership.

Wherever she went, Mother Teresa emphasized and insisted on the unity, love, peace, and joy that must exist in the life of the family. She was an adamant advocate for the family unit as a sacred creation. She was a tenacious opponent of abortion. She reminded everyone, on every occasion, that abortion was a crime against children, women, family, and life. She spoke up about this issue in her acceptance speech as winner of the Nobel Peace Prize in 1979, and also at the National Prayer Breakfast in Washington, D.C., in 1994 in the presence of the president and the Washington Establishment, many of whom held an opposite view on the subject.

Her fight for peace was equally bold. She went to the United Nations in 1985 and made her point about peace known to all the nations. No wonder she was introduced by the then-secretary general, Javier Pérez de Cuellar, with these words: "I present to you the most powerful woman in the world" (MTWL, 29).

Pope John Paul II, recognizing Mother Teresa's integrity, her charisma, and the qualities of her leadership, asked her on many occasions to contribute to his campaign for peace, prayer, holiness, the family, the right of the unborn child, and the union of all Christians. In a sense, she became "the Pope's ambassadress-at-large" (MTWL, 69). "I think," a Vatican prelate observed, "the future will show what a major revolution the Pope with the help of Mother Teresa has introduced. Both the Pope and Mother Teresa have defended the identity and dignity of women in a concentric way, calling on women to assume the function in society for defending life and the family and making sure that the sound values in modern society are a central part of the church, not marginal."[4]

Even though Mother Teresa was in contact with religious and civil authorities at the highest level who recognized the authenticity of her leadership, she was happiest in her daily work with the poor, the hungry, and the dying. This is where her focus was. She used her high-profile relationships to benefit the poorest of the poor, and then she disappeared behind them. She never took advantage of the situation for herself.

A genuine leader does not lead by force, wealth, fame, politics, a cunning mind, higher education, or an impressive résumé. A genuine leader leads by being true, trustworthy, and real. Leaders of this kind are charismatic. They inspire. People are transformed by contact with them. Mother Teresa was such a leader.

This is not to say she never stumbled or faced rejection or misunderstanding. It is a fact, for example, that not everyone, even in India, wanted a home for the destitute dying or a center for lepers in their neighborhoods. Even after settling in, the Missionaries of Charity were asked to leave. This happened in Northern Ireland and in Sri Lanka.

It is also a fact that Mother Teresa was friendly with public officials and private individuals whose values and conduct were contrary to her own. What is more, she accepted their charitable donations, regardless of their motives. In 1994, for example, she and her sisters were attacked very harshly for accepting donations from individuals like Haiti's exiled dictator Jean-Claude Duvalier. Mother Teresa's argument was that "she had no moral right to refuse donations given for the poor and miserable."[5]

Mother Teresa was also blamed for being, at times, too tough, too excessive in her austerity. It was reported, for example, that when she came to inaugurate the new house in San Francisco and found it too elegant and too "rich," she immediately demanded that the sisters get rid of the mattresses, carpets, and some other pieces of furniture, without any consideration for the donors' feelings. But she was not simply austere for the sake of austerity. She wanted her sisters to live exactly like the poor they served. As she said, "At the end of life we will not be judged by how many diplomas we have received, how much money we have made, how many great things we have done. We will be judged by 'I was hungry and you gave me to eat, I was naked and you clothed me, I was homeless and you took me in' " (WLB, 80).

Was Mother Teresa, in the end, just a rigid and domineering person, as some critical minds saw her? Father Bob Fabing, S.J., who met Mother Teresa more than seventy times during the last fourteen years of her life, did not think so. He attested the following: "I have found that when the needs of the poor were on the line, she was undeviating and very demanding. But I didn't find that she inspired fear. Her control was one of love. She inspired a generosity that was infectious."[6]

Probably the most serious criticism of Mother Teresa was that she did not work directly to change the structures and laws of society that would have helped to eradicate poverty. This is how she answered this concern: "I never look at the masses as my responsibility. I can love only one person at a time. I can feed only one person at a time.... Maybe if I didn't pick up that one person I wouldn't have picked up 42,000" (WLB, 79). On another occasion she said, "I never think in terms of a crowd, but of individual persons. If I thought in terms of crowds, I would never begin my work. I believe in the personal touch of one to one" (OW, 99).

Mother Teresa believed that "to know the problem of poverty intellectually is not to understand it" (LS, 55). She also believed that people were hungry and dying in the here and now. And, in the long run, she wanted to change the minds and hearts of people and convince them of justice and compassion. Then, she believed, people themselves would change the laws and structures of society. She and her sisters wanted to stay "outside politics." Their approach was to advance justice and peace in the most fundamental way possible, which is to re-affirm conspicuously and dauntlessly the inviolability of human dignity.

None of these criticisms, well founded or not, seriously affected the recognition of Mother Teresa's leadership. Genuine leaders know their limitations. But they also know how to look to God for answers and solutions. They let themselves be led by God. This is why Mother Teresa made such a difference in the world, drawing in her steps an army of followers throughout the world, showing them the path to God. She was a true spiritual master.

MOTHER TERESA:
A SPIRITUAL MASTER

Mother Teresa said, "It doesn't matter what we do or where we are as long as we remember that we belong to [Jesus], that we are his, that we are in love with him" (MLP, 91); "I belong entirely to the heart of Jesus" (SVS, 357). It was this relationship that defined her spiritual path.

Mother Teresa was not a philosopher who created a complex system. She was not a theologian who speculated about the mysteries of God and life. She was not a great writer who possessed the art of saying things in the most sophisticated way. She did not even seek to convince people of her beliefs. She simply lived her beliefs in the most simple way. She demonstrated that human beings — no matter who or what they are — when surrounded by love and caring, are closer to God and are therefore transformed and enabled to recover their dignity as human beings. For this reason she was more than a philosopher, a theologian, and a writer. She was a spiritual master.

What made her so? It was her radicalism, her loyalty to the word of God and the church, her integrated understanding for contemplative active life, her uncompromising stands on the issues, her clarity of vision and purpose, and her determination to go all the way.

Mother Teresa had an *unwavering, absolute, and total reliance on God's providence*. No worries were allowed in her heart, in her congregation, or in her work. She trusted totally, radically, all the way, no matter the consequences.

She was also marked by an *indubitable, unquestionable, and unconditional love for Jesus*. For her, Jesus was "My God... My spouse... My life... My only love... My all in all... My everything" (JWS, 129). She lived this love with her whole soul, heart, mind, and strength, truthfully, conscientiously, and confidently. When one loves so much, one follows the desires of the beloved. Her beloved Jesus said: "You shall love the Lord your God with all your heart, and with all your soul, and with all your mind" (Matt. 22:37). She lived this love concretely in the sick, the rejected, the unloved, and the poor, literally heeding the words of Jesus, "In so far as you did this to one of the least of these..., you did it to me" (Matt. 25:40, NJB).

Mother Teresa had a *boundless compassion for the poor and complete dedication to serving them*. When she won the Nobel Peace Prize, she used the $192,000 award, along with many other financial prizes and donations, to help her charitable work. For the poor she provided physical as well as psychological and spiritual care. She saw the poor unloved man or woman as Jesus in disguise. She was in love with Jesus wherever he was, without conditions, and without compromises. "Give until it hurts" (MLP, 62), she said. This "is the key to the paradox of blessedness in the world of poverty."[7]

But loving is not an easy task. It is not just a matter of good feeling or an intellectual exercise. Loving is another way of seeing things. It is a decision to carry out. It is incarnation and embodiment. It is the very earthiness of Jesus, not the speculation of theology and philosophy. In its essence, loving is intrinsically relational. It is the deepest relational reality of all. One cannot reach this reality alone. Mother Teresa certainly knew that. This is why she said: "My secret is quite simple. I pray" (LS, 1).

Mother Teresa had *unlimited confidence in prayer.* She said: "Prayer feeds the soul — as blood is to the body, prayer is to the soul — and it brings you closer to God" (SP, 7). She believed that alone, of herself, she could do nothing, but through prayers she could "move mountains," as Jesus promised, and she proved it.

She chose a *contemplative active lifestyle* to facilitate her prayer life, one in which her prayers became action and her actions became prayer. This integration of the two sides of spiritual life, the contemplative and the active, was for Mother Teresa her way to live the Gospel here and now. She bridged the two sides and proved concretely that holiness is not an escape from the world but an engaging cooperation in making a better world. She also proved that holiness is not for just a few, but for everyone.

In spite of overwhelming international attention to her personality and to her work, Mother Teresa retained her humble approach and her *simplicity.* Maybe this is why she and her sisters were so effective. They chose to be, in their lives, equal to the people they served: simple and poor. This was what they did because that was what Jesus did. Mother Teresa said: "We and the poor will depend entirely on divine providence both for material and spiritual needs" (MTR, 214). "Live simply" (MTR, 111).

This simple life extended beyond material poverty to an approach to life itself. As a result one of the most distinctive characteristics of Mother Teresa was her *astonishing, unceasing, radical and contagious joy.* As she observed, "Cheerfulness is indeed the fruit of the Holy Spirit and a clear sign of the Kingdom within" (JWS, 111). Therefore, joy is growth in holiness. This is how important joy is. Mother Teresa reminded us in the most tangible way that we find joy not in the change in our circumstances of life but when we find in depth what we are longing for. Simply, one is happy in God. As Mother Teresa said, "I am the happiest person in the world, because I am living with Jesus twenty-four hours a day" (MTLL, 80). This was apparent to all who met her. Father Andrew M. Greeley confirmed that "she was the happiest human being I had ever met."[8]

One might wonder, at this point, about Mother Teresa's mentors in her spiritual life. Who were her masters and heroes? Besides the mystics like St. John of the Cross and St. Teresa of Avila, two others had the biggest influence on her: the Virgin Mary and St. Thérèse of Lisieux.

Why Mary? Because Mary, said Mother Teresa, "can help us to love Jesus best; she is the one who can show us the shortest way to Jesus" (MTR, 112). The great devotion Mother Teresa had for Mary strengthened her relationship to Jesus. She learned from Mary's "Yes" to the angel. She learned from Mary how to love Jesus, how to be attentive to other's concerns, as she showed at the wedding at Cana; how to be of service, as when Mary helped her cousin Elizabeth with the baby. Mary was for Mother Teresa "the most beautiful among women, the greatest, the most humble, the purest, the holiest" (MTR, 107), and "the cause of our joy" (MTR, 106). She was the role model for Mother Teresa and all the Missionaries of Charity.

The other real bond was with St. Thérèse of Lisieux, the discoverer of "the little way." When the young Agnes Gonxha made her vows in 1931, she took St. Thérèse as her patron. She spelled her new name the Spanish way to avoid confusion with another sister, Marie-Thérèse Breen. But Mother Teresa explained that her patron was "not the big St. Teresa of Avila, but the little one" (MTB, 8), the saint of "the little way," of total childlike surrender to God.

We certainly can visualize Mother Teresa when we read something like this in St. Thérèse's *Story of a Soul:*

I understand so well that it is only love which makes us acceptable to God that this love is the only good I ambition. Jesus deigned to show me the road that leads to this Divine Furnace, and this road is the *surrender* of the little child who sleeps without fear in its Father's arms....

I understood that love comprised all vocations, that love was everything, that it embraced all times and places. ...In a word, that it was eternal....My vocation is love.[9]

"The little way" that teaches how to pray, how to trust in God's limitless love, how to live joyfully the true spiritual childlikeness, seems so simple. But it is not so. In fact, it challenges our very understanding of sanctity and questions the very righteousness of our human rules, the adequacy of our spiritual achievements, and the meaning of our pious activities. It corrects our vision by rooting our sanctity in the love of God and in the total surrender of our ordinary life to the divine providence.

Mother Teresa learned from Mary "the shortest way to Jesus" and from St. Thérèse of Lisieux "the little way" of childlike surrender to God. Thus, she defined her own way: "With Jesus, for Jesus, to Jesus" (MTR, 205). She showed that the most brilliant theologians, philosophers, and writers are not necessarily the professionals after all, but rather those who can make a difference in the lives of others by drawing them closer to God — thus living a fulfilled life.

MOTHER TERESA: A FULFILLED LIFE

It is remarkable to see how huge the interest in Mother Teresa is today. Books, articles, and videos are created by the dozens about her. Her order is flourishing. Her work is expanding. Her legacy continues.

Is this interest due to society's need for her works? Is it due to her personality and the interesting story of her life? Is it due to her organizational talents? These are all relevant factors, but there is more. Mother Teresa translated the Gospel into a language of action. She proved that holiness is possible, accessible, and imperative. She saw Christ in everyone without inquiring about their backgrounds. She was a living example of global ecumenism. And above all, she was happy. Her joy and the joy of her sisters were obvious. Malcolm Muggeridge describes them this way:

> Their life is tough and austere by worldly standards, certainly; yet I never met such delightful, happy women, or such an atmosphere of joy as they create. Mother Teresa, as she is fond of explaining, attaches the utmost importance to this joyousness. The poor, she says, deserve not just service and dedication, but also the joy that belongs to human love. This is what the sisters give them abundantly. (SBG, 37)

This joy is their only advertisement. And it works. When genuine joy radiates, it becomes contagious. Everyone becomes interested in having this kind of joy. One of the reasons Princess Diana of Wales was drawn to Mother Teresa was just that. Princess Diana had it all: youth, beauty, wealth, fame. She was mother of a future king, she had a fairy-tale wedding, and all those things of which a person can dream. But all this did not give her happiness. Mother Teresa, by contrast, lacked all of Diana's gifts of a worldly life, and yet she was "the happiest person in the world" (MTLL, 80). Like many of Mother Teresa's admirers, Diana too was evidently hungry for this kind of happiness. True love is the secret of this happiness, and this is what our world needs most. "The world," noticed Mother Teresa, "has never had such a need for love as it has today" (MTLL, 118).

Many of us — the number is increasing every day — are tired

of living lies. We long for truth, integrity, and real love. Mother Teresa is an inspiring, tested, and trustworthy companion to that road and to a better world. She brings back hope where hope was long gone. She inspires confidence, reliability, and a joy that is infectious.

Mother Teresa's life and the life of the Missionaries of Charity and their dedicated work of love, courage, and determination toward the most marginalized victims of our society pose some of the most profound questions to our civilization and way of life. Mother Teresa showed that it is possible to live the Gospel and that only one thing matters: holiness. Then everything falls in place, allowing God to work through each one of us and so to make of this world the best it can be. "The essential thing," Mother Teresa truly believed, "is not what we say, but what God says to us and through us" (MLP, 108).

When we leave this world, will we leave behind a legacy of love as Mother Teresa did? No matter what we do and no matter how many successes we are able to accumulate, if love is not there, no fulfillment is reached and no salvation is possible. True love is the only satisfying answer to human restlessness, and holiness is the only genuine fullness of life. Mother Teresa had it right.

For this reason she captured hearts, helped to heal minds and bodies, and transformed souls. For this reason she is rightly regarded as one of the most beloved and influential spiritual masters of our time.

NOTES

1. Barbara Crosette, "Pomp Pushes the Poorest from Mother Teresa's Last Rites," *New York Times International,* September 14, 1997, 14.

2. Quoted by Joanna Hurley, *Mother Teresa: A Pictorial Biography* (Philadelphia: Courage Books, 1997), 78.

3. "Mother Teresa's Mourners Throng to a Grieving Calcutta," *New York Times,* September 7, 1997, 6.

4. Quoted by Anne Sebba, *Mother Teresa: Beyond the Image* (New York: Doubleday, 1997), 261.

5. Subir Bhaumik and Meenakshi Ganguly, "Mother Teresa, 1910–1997, Seeker of Souls," *Time,* September 15, 1997, 83.

6. John L. Allen, Jr., "Fabing's Music Echoes in Teresa's Life, Death," *National Catholic Reporter,* October 17, 1997, 20.

7. Brother Angelo Devananda, in Introduction to JWS, xii.

8. Andrew M. Greeley, "The Happiest Human," *Newsweek,* September 22, 1997, 35.

9. *Story of a Soul: The Autobiography of St. Thérèse of Lisieux,* a new translation from the original manuscript by John Clarke, O.C.D. (Washington, D.C.: ICS Publications, 1971), 188, 194.

1

A Focused Life

†

Unless we discern, follow, and achieve our own particular destiny, we can never be happy. In modern times, a most striking example of this simple truth is Mother Teresa of Calcutta.

Mother Teresa heard her special call on a train trip. She listened carefully to it, and she focused fully on the caller, because she knew it was Jesus. She surrendered to his call totally and without reservation. She met Christ in the sick, the hungry, the outcast, the poorest of the poor, and the dying. She took his words seriously: "Truly I tell you, just as you did it to one of the least of these who are members of my family, you did it to me" (Matt. 25:40). This is what she did and how she lived.

GOD'S CALL

I was only twelve years old, living with my parents in Skopje, Yugoslavia, when I first sensed the desire to become a nun. At that time there were some very good priests who helped boys and girls follow their vocation, according to God's call. It was then that I realized that my call was to the poor.

Between twelve and eighteen years of age I lost the desire to become a nun. But at eighteen years of age I decided to leave my home and enter the Sisters of Loreto. Since then I have never

had the least doubt that I was right. It was God's will: he made
the choice.   —HJ, 39

At Loreto I was the happiest nun in the world. Leaving the
work I did there was a great sacrifice. What I did not have to
leave was being a religious sister.

The Sisters of Loreto were devoted to teaching, which is a
genuine apostolate for Christ. But my specific vocation, within
the religious vocation, was for the poorest poor. It was a call
from inside my vocation — like a second vocation. It was a command to resign Loreto, where I was happy, in order to serve the
poor in the streets.

In 1946, when I was going by train to Darjeeling for some
spiritual exercises, I sensed a call to renounce everything in
order to follow Christ in the poor suburbs, to serve among the
poorest poor. I knew that God wanted something from me.
                                                —HJ, 39–40

In the world there are some who struggle for justice and human
rights. We have no time for this because we are in daily and
continuous contact with men who are starving for a piece of
bread to put in their mouth and for some affection. Should I
devote myself to struggle for the justice of tomorrow or even
for the justice of today, the most needy people would die right
in front of me because they lack a glass of milk.

Nevertheless, I want to state clearly that I do not condemn
those who struggle for justice. I believe there are different op-
tions for the people of God. To me the most important is to
serve the neediest people.

Within the church some do one thing, others do a different
thing. What is important is that all of us remain united, each
one of us developing his own specific task.   —HJ, 113–14

A vocation is a gift of Christ. He has said, "I have chosen
you." Every vocation must really belong to Christ. The work

that we are called to accomplish is just a means to give concrete substance to our love for God.

Young women today are seeking something to which they can commit everything. They are convinced that a life of poverty, of prayer, of sacrifice — which will be of help to them in the service of their neighbor, of the poorest poor — is the answer to their desires, their aspirations, their hopes.

I think they see in our congregation this life of poverty, of prayer, and of sacrifice. In our work on behalf of the poorest poor they see carried into action the Lord's words, "I was hungry and you fed me; I was naked and you clothed me; I was homeless and you welcomed me" (see Matt. 25:35, 36). This is what we, in the anguish and sorrow of the poor, try to do for Christ.   —HJ, 121–22

Our vocation is to follow the lowliness of Christ. We remain right on the ground by living Christ's concern for the poorest and the lowliest and by being of immediate but effective service to them until they find some others who can help in a better and more lasting way.   —TS, 82

Our vocation is the conviction that "I belong to him." Because I belong to him, he must be free to use me. I must surrender completely.   —TS, 38

What is our vocation? What do we call vocation? Our vocation is Jesus. We have it in the Scripture very clearly: "I have called you by name, you are precious to me ... I have called you my friend. Water will not drown you." (Water symbolizes all these temptations of evil.) "I will give nations for you; you are precious." "How could a mother forget her child? Or a woman the child within her womb? But even if a mother could forget, I will never forget you. You are precious to me; you are carved in the palm of my hand."

Why are we here? We must have heard Jesus calling us

by name. We are like St. Paul. Once he realized the love of Christ, he cared about nothing else. He did not care whether he was scourged or put into prison. For him, only one thing was important: Jesus Christ....

God doesn't want one more congregation in the world — just three thousand nuns more. We have been created and chosen to proclaim his love so that people may see the wonderful works of God. I will never forget a man in Kalighat who observed a sister as she was taking care of a patient. The sister did not know she was being watched. Afterwards the man came to me and said: "Mother, I came here godless. Today I found God in that sister — the way she was looking at the sick person and taking care of him." This is what we have been created for — to proclaim Christ's love, to proclaim his presence.   — TS, 27–28

This is our mission: to make God present in the world of today by our life and witness.   — MTLL, 97

The specific purpose of our congregation is the conversion and sanctification of the poor who live in the slums or in colonies of outcasts; that is, to assist the sick and the dying, to care for the street children, to visit the beggars ... to work for the conversion and salvation of the poor.... To convert and sanctify is God's work.... To bring the light of Christ to the darkness of the hovels in the slums, we must bring our Lord where he has never gone before....   — MTLL, 111

A vocation is simply a call to belong entirely to Christ, with the conviction that nothing can separate me from his love. A vocation is an invitation to be always in love with God and to give witness to that love always and everywhere.   — MTLL, 26

A vocation is a gift from the Lord. Christ said: "I have chosen you.... " Young people today are searching for something to which they can give all or nothing.... To "renounce" means to offer my free will, my judgment, my life in a manifestation of faith; it means to love. An active love calls for suffering. Jesus showed his love by dying on the cross for us. True love will cost us a great deal of sacrifice....

I think that vocations are lacking today because there is little prayer in the family; also because there is too much wealth, too much comfort, not only in families but also in religious life....

The most important event that I have experienced in my life is my encounter with Christ. He is my support....Our yes to God must be without reservation.   —MTLL, 132–33

In our congregation we have sisters from every part of the world. Some of them come from families that are wealthy and very well off. When they come to us, they persevere and are content with our life. I myself ask them: "Why do you want to remain with us?" And for sure the immediate reply is: "Because of Jesus, and because of our poverty." They tell me: "Mother, we want only one wealth — Jesus — and we are happy to have found a congregation that is poor and depends entirely on divine providence."...My specific vocation is for the poor among the poorest of the poor. And it was not easy....A house was needed in which to gather the abandoned. I started to look for one....I walked and walked until I could go no farther. I then understood better how much the poor suffer; always in search of food, medicine, everything. The memory of the material comfort I enjoyed in the convent of Loreto was like a temptation for me. I prayed: "My God, by my free choice and for love of you I want to remain here and do whatever your divine will asks of me. The poor are my community. Their security is mine. Their health is mine. The new house will be the house of the poor."...We live and work for God through our consecration, striving to witness God's love to the poor, and especially to those who are suffering....Our vocation is holiness....We all have the duty of serving God wherever we are: in our family, at work, in school, in the hospital, wherever.   —MTLL, 28

If there are people who feel that God wants them to change the structures of society, that is something between them and their God. We must serve him in whatever way we are called. I am called to help the individual; to love each poor person. Not to deal with institutions. I am in no position to judge.

— GG, 42–43

The form of the call is not important. It is something between me and God. What is important is that God calls each one in a different way. There is no merit on our part. The important thing is to respond to the call. Just as in that difficult and dramatic moment even now I am sure that this is God's work, not mine. And since it is his work, I knew that the world would benefit by it.   — MTLW, 39

"A Missionary of Charity *must be a missionary of love.*" A missionary is one who is sent. God sent his Son. Today God sends us. Each one of us is sent by God. Why are we sent? We are sent to be his love among men, to bring his love and compassion to the poorest of the poor. We must not be afraid to love. A Missionary of Charity *must* be a missionary of love. Notice the words *"must be."* It is not that she should simply try to be. No, she *must be* a missionary of love. She is sent to *be* God's love.

— TS, 49

No Missionary of Charity is called to do big things. Our work sounds big because there are so many little things, but when you look at it, there is nothing to show — nothing. I was so happy to see a sister cleaning the toilets, because they were shining. She must have cleaned them with great love and done it in the presence of God.   — TS, 122–23

What delicate love God has had for the poor of the world to have created the Missionaries of Charity. You and I have been called by our name, because he loved us. Because you and I are somebody special to him — to be his heart to love him in the poor, his hands to serve him in the poorest of the poor. My children, how much love and care we must take of him — if only we were in love with him. Let us learn to pray the work to be able to be twenty-four hours with Jesus, to do it for Jesus and to Jesus. We need a pure heart, a heart that is filled with nothing but Jesus.   —TS, 156–57

We all have the duty to serve God where we are called to do so. I feel called to serve individuals, to love each human being. My calling is not to judge the institutions. I am not qualified to condemn anyone. I never think in terms of a crowd, but of individual persons.

If I thought in terms of crowds, I would never begin my work.

I believe in the personal touch of one to one.

If others are convinced that God wants them to change social structures, that is a matter for them to take up with God.

—OW, 99

If our work were just to wash and feed and give medicines to the sick, the center would have closed a long time ago. The most important thing in our centers is the opportunity we are offered to reach souls.   —OW, 109

We have the specific task of giving material and spiritual help to the poorest of the poor, not only the ones in the slums but those who live in any corner of the world as well.

To do this, we make ourselves live the love of God in prayer and in our work, through a life characterized by the simplicity and humility of the Gospel. We do this by loving Jesus in the bread of the Eucharist, and loving and serving him hidden under the painful guise of the poorest of the poor, whether their poverty is a material poverty or a spiritual one. We do this by

recognizing in them (and giving back to them) the image and
likeness of God.   —OW, 108

My vocation is grounded in belonging to Jesus, and in the
firm conviction that nothing will separate me from the love of
Christ. The work we do is nothing more than a means of transforming our love for Christ into something concrete. I didn't
have to find Jesus. Jesus found me and chose me. A strong vocation is based on being possessed by Christ. It means loving him
with undivided attention and faithfulness through the freedom
of poverty and total self-surrender through obedience. This is
the call of being a Missionary of Charity, being wholeheartedly
given over to serving the poorest of the poor. It means serving
Christ through his suffering appearance in the poor:

> He is the Life that I want to live.
> He is the Light that I want to radiate.
> He is the Way to the Father.
> He is the Love with which I want to love.
> He is the Joy that I want to share.
> He is the Peace that I want to sow.
> He is Everything to me.
> Without him, I can do nothing.
> —OHFL, 15–16

The reason why the vocation of the Missionary of Charity
brothers and sisters and their co-workers is so beautiful is that
it is a vocation for everyone. All of us have been given the opportunity to be completely possessed by Jesus. The work he has
entrusted to you and me is nothing more than putting our love
for him into action. What you do, I cannot do. What I do, you
cannot do. But, together, you and I can do something beautiful
for God.   —OHFL, 21

TOTAL SURRENDER

Total surrender consists in giving ourselves completely to God. Why must we give ourselves fully to God? Because God has given himself to us. If God, who owes nothing to us, is ready to impart to us no less than himself, shall we answer with just a fraction of ourselves? To give ourselves fully to God is a means of receiving God himself. I live for God and give up my own self and in this way induce God to live for me. Therefore, to possess God, we must allow him to possess our souls. How poor we would be if God had not given us the power of giving ourselves to him. How rich we are now. How easy it is to conquer God! We give ourselves to God; then God is ours and there can be nothing more ours than God. The money with which God repays our surrender is himself.   —TS, 36–37

Our total surrender will come today by surrendering even our sins so that we will be poor. "Unless you become a child you cannot come to me." You are too big, too heavy; you cannot be lifted up. We need humility to acknowledge our sin. The knowledge of our sin helps us to rise. I will get up and go to my Father.   —TS, 37

One thing Jesus asks of me: that I lean on him; that in him and only in him I put complete trust; that I surrender myself to him unreservedly. Even when all goes wrong and I feel as if I am a ship without a compass, I must give myself completely to him. I must not attempt to control God's action; I must not count the stages in the journey he would have me make. I must not desire a clear perception of my advance upon the road, must not know precisely where I am upon the way of holiness. I ask him to make a saint of me, yet I must leave to him the choice of the saintliness itself and still more the means which leads to it....

Total surrender involves loving trust. You cannot surrender totally unless you trust lovingly and totally. Jesus trusted his Father because he knew him, he knew of his love. "My Father and I are one." "I am not alone, the Father is with me." "Father, into your hands I commend my Spirit." Read St. John's Gospel and see how many times Jesus used the word "Father." Jesus came to reveal the Father. In the time of the Old Testament God was known as the God of fear, punishment, and anger. The coming of Jesus reverses this picture completely. God in the New Testament is the God of love, compassion, and mercy. That is why we can trust him fully — there is no more fear. This loving trust implies that we know the love of God and that we proclaim this love, compassion, and mercy everywhere we are sent. Today we reveal him.   —TS, 39–41

A Missionary of Charity is just a little instrument in the hands of God. We must try to keep it always like that — being just a small instrument in his hands. Very often I feel like a little pencil in God's hand. He does the writing; he does the thinking; he does the movement — I have only to be a pencil and nothing else.   —TS, 126

Providence always comes to our help. When the need is immediate, the intervention of providence is also immediate. It is not always a matter of huge amounts, but of what is needed at a given moment.

One time we had picked up a man for whom a rare medicine was needed. While we were wondering how we could get it, a man knocked at our door with an abundant sampler of medicines. Among them was the one we urgently needed.
                                                    —HJ, 43

We can sincerely muster our courage and say, "In him who is the source of my strength I have strength for everything" (Phil. 4:13).

According to this statement of St. Paul, you should trust in the success of your work, which is rather God's work, with the effectiveness and perfection of Jesus and through Jesus. Be assured that by yourselves you can do nothing and have nothing, except sin, weakness, and misery. All our natural gifts and those that come from grace have been gratuitously offered us by God.

—HJ, 111–12

We depend solely on divine providence. Christ has said that we are more important in his eyes than the flowers, the grass, and the birds. He is concerned for those we help.

We care for thousands of people in India and elsewhere, and up to now we have always had something to give. We have never been forced to dismiss anyone because of lack of space or food. God has always been present with his love and concern.

—HJ, 124

Jesus wants us to put all our trust in him. We have to renounce our desires in order to work for our own perfection. Even if we feel like a boat without a compass on the high seas, we are to commit ourselves fully to him, without trying to control his actions.

I cannot long for a clear perception of my progress along the route, nor long to know precisely where I am on the path of holiness. I ask Jesus to make me a saint. I leave it to him to choose the means that can lead me in that direction.

—HJ, 126

St. Thérèse, the Little Flower, explained surrender very beautifully when she said, "I am like a little ball in the hand of Jesus. He plays with me. He throws me away, puts me in the corner. And then like a little child who wants to see what is inside, he tears the ball apart and throws the pieces away." This is what a brother, a sister, has to be, the little ball in the hand of Jesus, who says to Jesus, "You can do whatever you want, as you want, when you want, as long as you want."   —JWS, 25

We must know exactly when we say yes to God what is in that yes. Yes means "I surrender," totally, fully, without any counting the cost, without any examination, "Is it all right? Is it convenient?" Our yes to God is without any reservations. That's what it is to be a contemplative. I belong to him so totally that there are no reservations. It doesn't matter what we feel.

—JWS, 27

To surrender means to offer him my free will, my reason, my own life in pure faith. My soul may be in darkness. Trial and suffering are the surest test of my blind surrender.

Surrender is also true love. The more we surrender, the more we love God and souls. If we really love souls, we must be ready to take their place, to take their sins upon us and expiate them in us by penance and continual mortification. We must be living holocausts, for the souls need us as such.   —JWS, 56

This complete surrender of self to God must secure for us perseverance in God's service, since by obedience we always do his most holy will and consequently obtain freedom from doubts, anxieties, and scruples.   —JWS, 107–8

Total surrender — for us, contemplative life means also a joyous and ardent response to his call to the most intimate union with him by:

- totally abandoning ourselves into his hands,

- yielding totally to his every movement of love, giving him supreme freedom over us to express his love as he pleases, with no thought of self,

- desiring with ardent desire all the pain and delight involved in that union.

It also means:

- to be a willing prisoner of his love, a willing victim of his wounded love, a living holocaust, and

- even if he cuts us to pieces, to cry out, "Every piece is yours."

—JWS, 110

Loving trust means for our contemplative life:

- an absolute, unconditional, and unwavering confidence in God our loving Father, even when everything seems to be a total failure,

- to look to him alone as our help and protector,

- to stop doubting and being discouraged, casting all our worries and cares on the Lord, and walking in total freedom,

- to be daring and absolutely fearless of any obstacle, knowing that nothing is impossible with God, and

- total reliance on our Heavenly Father with a spontaneous abandonment of the little children, totally convinced of our utter nothingness but trusting to the point of rashness with courageous confidence in his fatherly goodness.

—JWS, 110–11

If we really fully belong to God, then we must be at his disposal and we must trust in him. We must never be preoccupied with the future. There is no reason to be so. God is there.

Our dependence on divine providence is a firm and lively faith that God can and will help us. That he can is evident, because he is almighty; that he will is certain because he promised it in so many passages of Holy Scripture and because he is infinitely faithful to all his promises. Christ encourages us to have this confidence in these words: "Whatever you ask in prayer, believe that you have received it, and it will be yours" (RSV). The apostle St. Peter also commands us to throw all cares upon the Lord who provides for us. And why should God not care for us since he sent us his Son and with him all? St. Augustine says: "How can you doubt that God will give you good things since he vouchsafed to assume evil for you?"

This must give us confidence in the providence of God who preserves even the birds and the flowers. Surely if God feeds the young ravens which cry to him, if he nourishes the birds which neither sow nor reap nor gather into barns; if he vests the flowers of the field so beautifully, how much more will he care for men whom he has made in his own image and likeness and adopted as his children, if we only act as such, keep his commandments, and have confidence in him.

I don't want the work to become a business but to remain a work of love. I want you to have that complete confidence that God won't let us down. Take him at his word and seek first the kingdom of heaven, and all else will be added on.

—LS, 26–27

We are at his disposal. If he wants you to be sick in bed, if he wants you to proclaim his Word in the street, if he wants you to clean the toilets all day, that's all right, everything is all right. We must say, "I belong to you. You can do whatever you like." This is our strength, and this is the joy of the Lord.

—MTR, 137

We put our hands, our eyes, and our hearts at Christ's disposal, so that he will act through us.   —MTR, 156

Our total surrender to God means to be entirely at the disposal of the Father as Jesus and Mary were. In giving ourselves completely to God, because God has given himself to us, we are entirely at his disposal —

- to be possessed by him so that we may possess him;

- to take whatever he gives and to give whatever he takes with a big smile;

- to be used by him as it pleases him without being consulted;

- to offer him our free will, our reason, our whole life in pure faith, so that he may think his thoughts in our minds, do his work through our hands, and love with our hearts.

—MTR, 139

EXISTENTIAL CHRIST

It is very possible that you will find human beings, surely very near you, needing affection and love. Do not deny them these. Show them, above all, that you sincerely recognize that they are human beings, that they are important to you.

Who is that someone?

That person is Jesus himself: Jesus who is hidden under the guise of suffering! —OW, 84

Jesus continues to live his passion. He continues to fall, poor and hungry, just like he fell on the way to Calvary.

Are we at his side to volunteer to help him? Do we walk next to him with our sacrifice, with our piece of bread — real bread — to help him get over his weakness? —OW, 86

When we are caring for the sick and the needy, we are touching the body of the suffering Christ, and this touch makes us heroic; it helps us overcome the repugnance and the natural reaction that is in all of us. This is the eye of faith and of love, to see Christ in the sick and to serve him, sharing their suffering, everything.... Suffering is not a punishment. Jesus does not punish. Suffering is a sign, a sign that God loves us.... Through suffering, pain, the cross, sickness, and death, we arrive at life, at the resurrection.   —MTLL, 125

If our sisters did not see the face of Jesus in these unfortunate persons, this kind of work would be impossible.... We want them to know that there are persons who truly love them, and even more, that God loves them very much....

All my time belongs to others, because in dedicating myself with all my heart to the suffering, it is Jesus whom we serve in his disfigured face, for he himself has said: "You have done it for me."...

Our criterion for assistance is not one's belief, but one's need. All are the body of Christ; all are Christ under the appearance of those in need of assistance and love, and they have a right to receive it.   —MTLL, 34–35

All that we do is for Jesus, with Jesus and offered to Jesus.

For Jesus: Our whole life is directed to him, to his service; we live only for him, to love and serve him, to make him known and loved.

With Jesus: He gives us the strength, the comfort, the happiness of working for him; he accompanies us on our way; he leads and guides us; we are with Jesus on the road to Emmaus, where we have recognized him.

Offered to Jesus: We serve him in our neighbor; we see him in the poor; we care for him in the sick; we comfort him in our brothers and sisters who suffer.   —MTLL, 49–50

My greatest reward is to love Jesus. He is everything to me. He is my life, my love, my recompense, my all.   —MTLL, 66

You are God.
You are true God from true God.
Generated not created.
Of the selfsame substance of the Father.

You are the Second Person of the most holy Trinity.
You are one in being with the Father.
You are with the Father from all eternity.
All things were created by you and the Father.
You are the Beloved Son in whom the Father is well
	pleased.
You are the Son of Mary,
conceived by the Holy Spirit in her virginal womb.
You were born in Bethlehem.
You were wrapped in swaddling clothes by Mary
and placed in a manger filled with straw.
You are an ordinary man without much education,
and the educated class in Israel judges you.
Jesus is: the Word made flesh...
the bread of life,
the victim immolated for our sins on the cross,
the sacrifice offered for the sins of the world
and for my sins in the Holy Mass,
the word to be proclaimed,
the truth to be revealed,
the way to be followed,
the light to illumine,
the life to live,
the love to be loved,
the hungry person to be fed,
the thirsty person given drink,
the naked one to clothe,
the homeless to receive shelter,
the sick to be cured,
the abandoned to be loved,
the outcast to be welcomed,
the leper whose wounds are bathed,
the beggar to whom a smile is given,
the drunkard who needs to be listened to,
the mentally disturbed who needs to be protected,

the infant who needs to be held in our arms,
the blind person who needs to be led by the hand,
the mute for whom someone must speak,
the crippled with whom one walks,
the drug addict who needs help,
the prostitute who needs to be taken off the street and
     listened to,
the prisoner who needs to be visited,
the aged person who needs to be taken care of.
                                            —MTLL, 67

My secret is Jesus and his great love for us, prayer and meditation, the daily hour of adoration, our religious vows. My motto
is: Everything for Jesus; all for Jesus through Mary. Look at the
five fingers of my hand. He has made all this for me! Remember
to look at your hand and your five fingers, every morning and
night, and during the examination of conscience. What have I
done for Jesus?   —MTLL, 68

We do not try to impose our faith on others. We try to act in
such a way that Christ will make his light and his life shine
forth in us and, through us, in the world.   —MTLL, 68

Actually we are touching Christ's body in the poor. In the poor
it is the hungry Christ that we are feeding, it is the naked Christ
that we are clothing, it is to the homeless Christ that we are
giving shelter.
    It is not just hunger for bread or the need of the naked for
clothes or of the homeless for a house made of bricks. Even the
rich are hungry for love, for being cared for, for being wanted,
for having someone to call their own.   —GG, 39

If sometimes our poor people have had to die of starvation, it
is not because God didn't care for them, but because you and I

didn't give, were not instruments of love in the hands of God, to give them that bread, to give them that clothing; because we did not recognize him, when once more Christ came in distressing disguise — in the hungry man, in the lonely man, in the homeless child, and seeking for shelter.

God has identified himself with the hungry, the sick, the naked, the homeless; hunger, not only for bread, but for love, for care, to be somebody to someone; nakedness, not of clothing only, but nakedness of that compassion that very few people give to the unknown; homelessness, not only just for a shelter made of stone, but that homelessness that comes from having no one to call your own. —GG, 24–25

Because we cannot see Christ we cannot express our love to him; but our neighbors we can always see, and we can do for them what, if we saw him, we would like to do for Christ....

Today, the same Christ is in people who are unwanted, unemployed, uncared for, hungry, naked, and homeless. They seem useless to the state and to society; nobody has time for them. It is you and I as Christians, worthy of the love of Christ if our love is true, who must find them, and help them; they are there for the finding. —GG, 28

Today, once again, when Jesus comes among us, his own do not know him.

He comes in the repugnant bodies of the poor, but he comes also in the rich, who are suffocated by their wealth.

He comes in the loneliness of their hearts, and when there is no one to love them.

Jesus also comes to you and to me, but frequently, very frequently, we pass him by. —MTLL, 65

I remember one of our sisters, who had just graduated from the university. She came from a well-to-do family that lived outside of India. According to our rule, the very next day after joining our society, the postulants must go to the home for the dying destitute in Calcutta. Before this sister went, I told her, "You saw the priest during the Mass, with what love, with what delicate care he touched the body of Christ. Make sure you do the same thing when you get to the home, because Jesus is there in a distressing disguise."

So she went, and after three hours, she came back. That girl from the university, who had seen and understood so many things, came to my room with such a beautiful smile on her face. She said, "For three hours I've been touching the body of Christ!"

And I said, "What did you do? What happened?"

She said, "They brought a man from the street who had fallen into a drain and had been there for some time. He was covered with maggots and dirt and wounds. And though I found it very difficult, I cleaned him, and I knew I was touching the body of Christ!"

She knew!   —HW, 55

Hungry for love, He looks at you. Thirsty for kindness, He begs of you. Naked for loyalty, He hopes in you. Homeless for shelter in your heart, He asks of you. Will you be that one to Him?
                                                       —HW, 56

One day I was walking down the street in London, and I saw a tall, thin man sitting on the corner, all huddled up, looking most miserable.

I went up to him, shook his hand, and asked him how he was. He looked up at me and said, "Oh! After such a long, long time I feel the warmth of a human hand!" And he sat up.

There was such a beautiful smile on his face because somebody was kind to him. Just shaking his hand had made him feel like somebody.

For me, he was Jesus in a distressing disguise. I gave him the feeling of being loved by somebody, the joy of being loved.

Somebody loves us, too — God himself. We have been created to love and to be loved. —HW, 67–68

Dearest Lord, may I see you today and every day in the person of your sick, and, while nursing them, minister unto you.

Though you hide yourself behind the unattractive disguise of the irritable, the exacting, the unreasonable, may I still recognize you and say: "Jesus, my patient, how sweet it is to serve you."

Lord, give me this seeing faith, then my work will never be monotonous. I will ever find joy in humoring the fancies and gratifying the wishes of all poor sufferers.

O beloved sick, how doubly dear you are to me, when you personify Christ; and what a privilege is mine to be allowed to tend you.

Sweetest Lord, make me appreciative of the dignity of my high vocation, and its many responsibilities. Never permit me to disgrace it by giving way to coldness, unkindness, or impatience. And O God, while you are Jesus, my patient, deign also to be to me a patient Jesus, bearing with my faults, looking only to my intention, which is to love and serve you in the person of each of your sick.

Lord, increase my faith, bless my efforts and work, now and for evermore. Amen. —SBG, 53–54

I do not agree with the big way of doing things. To us what matters is an individual. To get to love the person we must come in close contact with him. If we wait till we get the numbers, then we will be lost in the numbers. And we will never be able to show that love and respect for the person. I believe in person to person; every person is Christ for me, and since there is only one Jesus, that person is only one person in the world for me at that moment. —SBG, 90–91

At the end of life we will not be judged by how many diplomas we have received, how much money we have made, how many great things we have done.

We will be judged by "I was hungry and you gave me to eat, I was naked and you clothed me, I was homeless and you took me in."

Hungry not only for bread — but hungry for love,

Naked not only for clothing — but naked of human dignity and respect,

Homeless not only for want of a room of bricks — but homeless because of rejection.

This is Christ in distressing disguise.   — WLB, 80

Jesus comes to meet us. To welcome him, let us go to meet him.

He comes to us in the hungry, the naked, the lonely, the alcoholic, the drug addict, the prostitute, the street beggars.

He may come to you or me in a father who is alone, in a mother, in a brother, or in a sister.

If we reject them, if we do not go out to meet them, we reject Jesus himself.   — OW, 29

The important thing is not to do a lot or to do everything. The important thing is to be ready for anything, at all times; to be convinced that when serving the poor, we really serve God.

                                                        — OW, 29

2

A Prayerful Life

†

To be able to live Jesus' words thoroughly was not easy, not even for Mother Teresa. She needed help. She prayed for divine help. She wanted to pray twenty-four hours each day. By practicing exterior and interior silence and by listening to God who spoke to the silence of her heart, she was able to be an active contemplative in the world and to transform her daily active life into unceasing prayer.

CENTRALITY OF PRAYER

Love to pray. Feel often during the day the need for prayer, and take trouble to pray. Prayer enlarges the heart until it is capable of containing God's gift of himself. Ask and seek, and your heart will grow big enough to receive him and keep him as your own.   — GG, 75

Does your mind and your heart go to Jesus as soon as you get up in the morning? This is prayer, that you turn your mind and heart to God. In your times of difficulties, in sorrows, in sufferings, in temptations, and in all things, where did your mind and heart turn first of all? How did you pray? Did you take the trouble to turn to Jesus and pray, or did you seek consolations?

Has your faith grown? If you do not pray, your faith will leave you. All those priests and religious who left first stopped praying and then lacked faith to go on.

Ask the Holy Spirit to pray in you. Learn to pray, love to pray, and pray often. Feel the need to pray and to want to pray.

If you have learned how to pray, then I am not afraid for you. If you know how to pray, then you will love prayer — and if you love to pray, then you will pray. Knowledge will lead to love and love to service.   —TS, 99

If you don't pray, your presence will have no power, your words will have no power. If you pray, you will be able to overcome all the tricks of the devil. Don't believe all the thoughts that he puts into your mind.   —TS, 101

There is only one powerful prayer; there is only one voice that rises up from the face of the earth; it is the voice of Christ. The more we receive in our silent prayer, the more we can give in our active life.   —MTLL, 45

When the disciples asked Jesus to teach them how to pray, he answered: "When you pray, say: Our Father..." He did not teach them any particular method or technique. He simply said that we should pray to God as our Father, as a loving Father. I have said to the bishops that the disciples had seen the master pray many times, even for entire nights. The people should see you pray and recognize you as men of prayer. Then they will listen to you when you speak to them about prayer.... We have such a need of prayer in order to be able to see Christ in the afflicted countenances of the poorest of the poor.... Speak to God; let God speak to you; let Jesus pray in you. To pray means to speak with God. He is my Father. Jesus is my all.
                                          —MTLL, 46

If you want to pray better, you should pray more.... Prayer helps us to know and do the will of God.... God is a friend of silence. We have to find God, but we cannot find him in the midst of noise and agitation.... If we really want to pray, we must above all dispose ourselves to listen, because in the silence of the heart the Lord speaks. — MTLL, 47

It is not possible to engage in the direct apostolate without being a soul of prayer. We must be aware of oneness with Christ, as he was aware of oneness with his Father. Our activity is truly apostolic only insofar as we permit him to work in us and through us with his power, with his desire, with his love.
— GG, 74

The Mass is the spiritual food that sustains me, without which I could not get through one single day or hour in my life; in the Mass we have Jesus in the appearance of bread, while in the slums we see Christ and touch him in the broken bodies, in the abandoned children. — GG, 76

The apostles asked Jesus to teach them to pray, and he taught them the beautiful prayer, "Our Father." I believe each time we say the "Our Father," God looks at his hands, where he has carved us — "I have carved you on the palm of my hand" — he looks at his hands, and he sees us there. How wonderful the tenderness and love of God!

Where can I learn to pray? Jesus taught us: "Pray like this: Our Father ... thy will be done ... forgive us as we forgive." It is so simple yet so beautiful. If we pray the "Our Father," and live it, we will be holy. Everything is there: God, myself, my neighbor. All this comes from a humble heart, and if we have this we will know how to love God, to love self, and to love our neighbor.

This is not complicated, and yet we complicate our lives

so much, by so many additions. Just one thing counts: to be humble, to pray.   —HW, 100

After the sisters have finished their day—carrying out their service of love in the company of Jesus, and through Jesus — we have an hour of prayer and of eucharistic adoration. Throughout the day we have been in contact with Jesus through his image of sorrow in the poor and the lepers. When the day ends, we come in contact with him again in the tabernacle by means of prayer. The tabernacle is the guarantee that Jesus has set his tent among us.

Every moment of prayer, especially before our Lord in the tabernacle, is a sure, positive gain. The time we spend in having our daily audience with God is the most precious part of the whole day.   —HW, 103–4

Prayer is nothing but being in the family, being one with the Father in the Son to the Holy Spirit. The love of the Father for his Son—the Holy Spirit. And the love, our love for the Father, through Jesus, his Son, filled with the Holy Spirit, is our union with God, and the fruit of that union with God, the fruit of that prayer — what we call prayer. We have given that name but actually prayer is nothing but that oneness with Christ.

As St. Paul has said, "I live no longer I, but Christ lives in me." Christ prays in me, Christ works in me, Christ thinks in me, Christ looks through my eyes, Christ speaks through my words, Christ works with my hands, Christ walks with my feet, Christ loves with my heart. St. Paul's prayer was, "I belong to Christ and nothing will separate me from the love of Christ." It was that oneness: oneness with God, oneness with the Master in the Holy Spirit.

And if we really want to pray we must first learn to listen, for in the silence of the heart God speaks. And to be able to hear that silence, to be able to hear God we need a clean heart, for a clean heart can see God, can hear God, can listen to God; and then only from the fullness of our heart can we speak to God. But we cannot speak unless we have listened, unless we have made that connection with God in the silence of our heart.

And so prayer is not meant to be a torture, is not meant to make us feel uneasy, is not meant to trouble us. It is something to look forward to, to talk to my Father, to talk to Jesus, the one to whom I belong: body, soul, mind, heart.

And when times come when we can't pray, it is very simple: if Jesus is in my heart let him pray, let me allow him to pray in me, to talk to his Father in the silence of my heart. Since I cannot speak — he will speak; since I cannot pray — he will pray. That's why often we should say: "Jesus in my heart, I believe in your faithful love for me, I love you." And often we should be in that unity with him and allow him, and when we have nothing to give — let us give him that nothingness. When we cannot pray — let us give that inability to him. There is one more reason to let him pray in us to the Father. Let us ask him to pray in us, for no one knows the Father better than he. No one can pray better than Jesus. And if my heart is pure, if in my heart Jesus is alive, if my heart is a tabernacle of the living God to sanctify in grace: Jesus and I are one. He prays in me, he thinks in me, he works with me and through me, he uses my tongue to speak, he uses my brain to think, he uses my hands to touch him in the broken body.

And for us who have the precious gift of Holy Communion every day, that contact with Christ is our prayer; that love for Christ, that joy in his presence, that surrender to his love is our prayer. For prayer is nothing but that complete surrender, complete oneness with Christ.

And this is what makes us contemplatives in the heart of the world, for we are twenty-four hours then in his presence: in the hungry, in the naked, in the homeless, in the unwanted, unloved, uncared for; for Jesus said: "Whatever you do to the least of my brethren, you do it to me."

Therefore doing it to him, we are praying the work; for in doing it with him, doing it for him, doing it to him we are loving him; and in loving him we come more and more into that oneness with him and we allow him to live his life in us. And this living of Christ in us is holiness.

> (Excerpted from talk of June 8, 1980, Berlin)
> —SVS, 426–27

The beginning of prayer is silence ... God speaking in the silence of the heart. And then we start talking to God from the fullness of the heart. And he listens.

The beginning of prayer is Scripture.... We listen to God speaking. And then we begin to speak to him again from the fullness of our heart. And he listens.

That is really prayer. Both sides listening and both sides speaking.   —WLB, 40

I believe that politicians spend too little time on their knees. I am convinced that they would be better politicians if they were to do so.   —OW, 7

There are some people who, in order not to pray, use as an excuse the fact that life is so hectic that it prevents them from praying.

This cannot be.

Prayer does not demand that we interrupt our work, but that we continue working as if it were a prayer.

It is not necessary to always be meditating, nor to consciously experience the sensation that we are talking to God, no matter how nice this would be. What matters is being with him, living in him, in his will. To love with a pure heart, to love everybody, especially to love the poor, is a twenty-four-hour prayer.   —OW, 7

Prayer is not asking. Prayer is putting oneself in the hands of God, at his disposition, and listening to his voice in the depths of our hearts. —OW, 9

Prayer, to be fruitful, must come from the heart and must be able to touch the heart of God. See how Jesus taught his disciples to pray. Call God your Father; praise and glorify his name. Do his will as the saints do it in heaven; ask for daily bread, spiritual and temporal; ask for forgiveness of your own sins and that you may forgive others, and also for the grace not to give in to temptations and for the final grace to be delivered from the evil that is in us and around us. —JWS, 3

We should be professionals in prayer. The apostles understood this very well. When they saw that they might be lost in a multitude of works, they decided to give themselves to continual prayer and to the ministry of the word. We have to pray on behalf of those who do not pray. —JWS, 3

In reality, there is only one true prayer, only one substantial prayer: Christ himself. There is only one voice which rises above the face of the earth: the voice of Christ. The voice reunites and coordinates in itself all the voices raised in prayer. —JWS, 4

Perfect prayer does not consist in many words but in the fervor of the desire which raised the heart to Jesus. Jesus has chosen us to be souls of prayer. The value of our actions corresponds exactly to the value of the prayer we make, and our actions are fruitful only if they are the true expression of earnest prayer. We must fix our gaze on Jesus, and if we work together with Jesus we will do much better. We get anxious and restless because we try to work alone, without Jesus. —JWS, 4

Often our prayers do not produce results because we have not fixed our mind and heart on Christ, through whom our prayers can ascend to God. Often a deep fervent look at Christ may make the most fervent prayer. "I look at him and he looks at me" is the most perfect prayer.   —JWS, 4

Our prayers are mostly vocal prayers; they should be burning words coming forth from the furnace of a heart filled with love. In these prayers, speak to God with great reverence and confidence. Pray with folded hands, downcast eyes, and lifted hearts, and your prayers will become like a pure sacrifice offered unto God. Do not drag or run ahead; do not shout or keep silent but devoutly, with great sweetness, with natural simplicity, without any affectation, offer your praise to God with the whole of your heart and soul.

We must know the meaning of the prayers we say and feel the sweetness of each word to make these prayers of great profit; we must sometimes meditate on them and often during the day find our rest in them.   —JWS, 8

SILENCE

If we will only learn silence, we will learn two things: to pray and to be humble. You cannot love unless you have humility, and you cannot be humble if you do not love. From the silence of the heart God speaks. There is no silence if there are things that have got inside.   —TS, 105

If we are careful of silence it will be easy to pray and to pray fervently. There is so much talk, so much repetition, so much carrying of tales in words and in writing. Our prayer life suffers so much because our hearts are not silent, for as you know "only in the silence of the heart, God speaks." Only after we have listened can we speak from the fullness of our hearts.
                          —TS, 107–8

A true interior life makes the active life burn with fervor and consume everything. This enables us to meet God in the darkest corners of the slums, in the saddest misery of the poor. It puts us in contact with the naked God-man on the cross; sad, despised by all, a man of sorrows, disdained like a worm.... And it is precisely because of this that we have such a great need for silence; the silence of humility, of charity; silence of the eyes and ears and tongue. Without this, the life of prayer does not exist. Silence leads to charity, and charity to humility. God speaks to us in silence, in prayer, in adoration, in the interior life. For that reason I insist on recommending silence. Silence of the tongue teaches us to speak of Christ and makes it possible for Christ to speak to us. Silence of the eyes enables us to see God. Our eyes are like two windows through which Christ can enter the world.

Sometimes we must have the courage to remain closed. We observe the silence of the heart, like the Blessed Virgin, who kept everything in her heart. Prayerful souls are souls of great silence. We cannot place ourselves in the presence of God without committing ourselves to interior and exterior silence. God is a friend of silence; he speaks to us in silence. We must find God, but God cannot be found in noise, distractions, or agitation.... If we are not able to accept ourselves and others, how can we communicate with God? The more we receive from our silent prayer, the more we can give in our active life. Silence gives us a clear vision of things.... The essential thing is not what we say, but what God says to us, and to others through us. Jesus waits for us in the silence of the tabernacle; he listens to us and he speaks to us; he loves us and makes us capable of loving him and of bearing witness of him to the world.   — MTLL, 82

If you face God in prayer and silence, God will speak to you. Then you will know that you are nothing. It is only when you realize your nothingness, your emptiness, that God can fill you with himself. Souls of prayer are souls of great silence.

There is a very holy priest, who is also one of the best theologians in India right now. I know him very well, and I said to him, "Father, you talk all day about God. How close you must be to God!" And you know what he said to me? He said, "I may be talking much *about* God, but I may be talking very little *to* God." And then he explained, "I may be rattling off so many words and may be saying many good things, but deep down I do not have the time to listen. Because in the silence of the heart, God speaks." ...

We cannot put ourselves directly in the presence of God if we do not practice internal and external silence.

In silence we will find new energy and true unity. Silence gives us a new outlook on everything.

The essential thing is not what we say but what God says to us and through us. In that silence, he will listen to us; there he will speak to our soul, and there we will hear his voice.

Listen in silence because if your heart is full of other things you cannot hear the voice of God. But when you have listened to the voice of God in the stillness of your heart, then your heart is filled with God.

The contemplatives and ascetics of all ages and religions have sought God in the silence and solitude of the desert, forest, and mountains. Jesus himself spent forty days in the desert and the mountains, communing for long hours with the Father in the silence of the night.

We too are called to withdraw at certain intervals into deeper silence and aloneness with God, together as a community as well as personally. To be alone with him — not with our books, thoughts, and memories but completely stripped of everything — to dwell lovingly in his presence, silent, empty, expectant, and motionless. We cannot find God in noise or agitation.

In nature we find silence — the trees, flowers, and grass grow in silence. The stars, the moon, and the sun move in silence.

Silence of the heart is necessary so you can hear God everywhere — in the closing of a door, in the person who needs you, in the birds that sing, in the flowers, in the animals.

What is essential is not what we say but what God tells us and what he tells others through us. In silence he listens to us; in silence he speaks to our souls. In silence we are granted the privilege of listening to his voice....

To make possible true inner silence, practice:

Silence of the eyes, by seeking always the beauty and goodness of God everywhere, closing them to the faults of others and to all that is sinful and disturbing to the soul;

Silence of the ears, by listening always to the voice of God and to the cry of the poor and the needy, closing them to all other voices that come from fallen human nature, such as gossip, tale-bearing, and uncharitable words;

Silence of the tongue, by praising God and speaking the life-giving Word of God that is the Truth, that enlightens and inspires, brings peace, hope, and joy, and by refraining from self-defense and every word that causes darkness, turmoil, pain, and death;

Silence of the mind, by opening it to the truth and knowledge of God in prayer and contemplation, like Mary who pondered the marvels of the Lord in her heart, and by closing it to all untruths, distractions, destructive thoughts, rash judgments, false suspicions of others, revengeful thoughts, and desires;

Silence of the heart, by loving God with our heart, soul, mind, and strength and one another as God loves, and avoiding all selfishness, hatred, envy, jealousy, and greed....

I shall keep the silence of my heart with greater care, so that in the silence of my heart I hear his words of comfort and from the fullness of my heart I comfort Jesus in the distressing disguise of the poor. For in the silence and purity of the heart God speaks.   — HW, 19–23

"God is the friend of silence. His language is silence." Be still and know that I am God. He requires us to be silent to discover him. In the silence of the heart, he speaks to us.

Jesus spent forty days before beginning his public life in silence. He often retired alone, spent the night on the mountain in silence and prayer. He who spoke with authority spent his early life in silence.

We need silence to be alone with God, to speak to him, to listen to him, to ponder his words deep in our hearts. We need to be alone with God in silence to be renewed and to be transformed. Silence gives us a new outlook on life. In it we are filled with the grace of God himself, which makes us do all things with joy.   —TS, 108

Silence gives us a new outlook on everything. We need silence to be able to touch souls. The essential thing is not what we say but what God says to us and through us. Jesus is always waiting for us in silence. In that silence, he will listen to us, there he will speak to our soul, and there we will hear his voice.

The interior silence is very difficult, but we must make the effort to pray. In silence we will find new energy and true unity. The energy of God will be ours to do all things well, and so will the unity of our thoughts with his thoughts, the unity of our prayers with his prayers, the unity of our actions with his actions, of our life with his life. All our words will be useless unless they come from within. Words which do not give the light of Christ increase the darkness.   —JWS, 2

This is what we have to learn right from the beginning, to listen to the voice of God in our heart, and then in the silence of the heart God speaks. Then from the fullness of our hearts, our mouth will have to speak. That is the connection. That is a Universal Brother of the Word. In the silence of the heart, God speaks and you have to listen. Then in the fullness of your heart, because it is full of God, full of love, full of compassion, full of faith, your mouth will speak. That's a true Brother of the Word.

Listen in silence, because if your heart is full of other things you cannot hear the voice of God. But when you have listened to the voice of God in the stillness of your heart, then your heart is filled with God, like our Lady full of grace. And then from the fullness of the heart the mouth will speak.   —JWS, 67–68

The apostles say, "We will devote ourselves to prayer and to the ministry of the word" (Acts 6:4, RSV). The more we receive in our silent prayer, the more we will be able to give in our active life. Silence gives us a new vision of things. We need that silence in order to get through to souls. What is essential is not what we say but what God tells us and what he tells others through us.

Jesus always waits for us in silence. In silence he listens to us; in silence he speaks to our souls. In silence we are granted the privilege of listening to his voice.   —MTR, 23

Our silence is a joyful and God-centered silence; it demands of us constant self-denial and plunges us into the deep silence of God where aloneness with God becomes a reality. —MTR, 25

To foster and maintain a prayerful atmosphere of exterior silence we shall —

- respect certain times and places of more strict silence;

- move about and work prayerfully, quietly, and gently;

- avoid at all costs all unnecessary speaking and notice;

- speak, when we have to, softly, gently, saying just what is necessary;

- look forward to profound silence as a holy and precious time, a withdrawal into the living silence of God.

          —MTR, 25

> Silence of our eyes.
> Silence of our ears.
> Silence of our mouths.
> Silence of our minds.
> Silence of our hearts.

For in the silence of the hearts God will speak. Give Jesus these five silences as a token of your gratitude.   —MTR, 25

You will never learn to pray until you keep silence:

> The fruit of silence is faith.
> The fruit of faith is prayer.
> The fruit of prayer is love.
> The fruit of love is service.
> And the fruit of service is silence.
>   —MTR, 25–26

Silence of the heart, not only of the mouth — that too is necessary. Then you can hear God everywhere: in the closing of the door, in the person who needs you, in the birds that sing, in the flowers, the animals — that silence which is wonder and praise. Why? Because God is everywhere, and you can see and hear him. That crow is praising God. That stupid crow — I can hear it well. We can see and hear God in that crow, but we cannot see and hear him if our heart is not clean.   —MTR, 26

Mary can teach us silence — how to keep all things in our hearts as she did, to pray in the silence of our hearts.   —LS, 22

Man needs silence.

To be alone or together looking for God in silence.

There it is that we accumulate the inward power which we distribute in action, put in the smallest duty, and spend in the severest hardships that befall us.

Silence came before creation, and the heavens were spread without a word.

Christ was born in the dead of night; and though there has been no power like his, "He did not strive nor cry, neither was his voice heard in the streets."

Once I was asked by someone what I consider most important in the training of the sisters. I answered:

Silence. Interior and exterior silence. Silence is essential in a religious house. The silence of humility, of charity, the silence of the eyes, of the ears, of the tongue. There is no life of prayer without silence.   —MLP, 108

CONTEMPLATION IN ACTION

We are active contemplatives in the world; we live entirely for Jesus. We find him and love and serve him first of all in the Eucharist, in prayer, in meditation, and then in persons who are suffering. If it were not for our faith, our love and service for our neighbor would be impossible.   —MTLL, 40

Action without meditation, without prayer and a spiritual life, is suicide for our faith and love. If you are supposed to bring Jesus to others, how much you must live in him, love him, and be close to him.... Today Jesus continues to suffer in you, in me, in the youth of the world. He is reliving his passion. To recognize this means to have faith, to love, to bear witness of Jesus to others.   —MTLL, 41

To work or live without love is a form of slavery. The church wants a renewal of herself in the world of today. But a renewal is not simply a change of clothing, something purely external; it is primarily an interior, radical change of the human heart by the grace of God.   —MTLL, 78

Prayer is not a flight from one's daily active life; much less is it a flight from oneself, from others, and from the world. It is a very authentic search for the true face of others and of God under the impetus of love and faith, which enables us to discover, understand, and more readily accept who we are, who others are, who God is, and what the meaning is of our life and work, and all that we are and do.   — MTLL, 78–79

Throughout the whole world there is a terrible longing, a terrible hunger for love, for God. There can be no interior life, no communion among brothers and sisters, without the practice of prayer. To be fruitful, prayer must come from the heart and be capable of touching the heart of God. See how Jesus taught his disciples to pray. Call God your Father; praise and glorify his name. Often our prayers, like everything else in our lives, are superficial. We have not fastened our mind and heart to Jesus, through whom our prayers can rise to God. Sometimes a fervent glance at Jesus can make our prayer more fervent. I look at him, and he looks at me; that is a perfect prayer.... My work does not distract me from God. When the sisters travel around, the poor do not ask them for clothing or for something to eat. They only say: "Teach us the word of God...." I have often thought that it would be nice to go off and live with the contemplative sisters, to live a life that is totally separated from the world, to simply be with Jesus. But then I realized that I can be like that even when traveling around the world, working and praying. Now I am the happiest person in the world, because I am living with Jesus twenty-four hours a day.... As to the poor of the world, I would say that they all want to feel that they have a Father in heaven, a Father who loves them.

                                              — MTLL, 80

By contemplation the soul draws directly from the heart of God the graces that the active life must distribute.

    We [the Missionaries of Charity] are called to be contemplatives in the heart of the world by:

Seeking the face of God in everything, everyone, everywhere, all the time, and his hand in every happening;

Seeing and adoring the presence of Jesus, especially in the lowly appearance of bread, and in the distressing disguise of the poor.

Our life of contemplation must retain the following characteristics:

Being missionaries: by going out physically or in spirit in search of souls all over the world.

Being contemplatives: by gathering the whole world at the very center of our hearts where the Lord abides, and allowing the pure water of divine grace to flow plentifully and unceasingly from the source itself, on the whole of his creation.

Being universal: by praying and contemplating with all and for all, especially with and for the spiritually poorest of the poor.

Another aspect of our life of contemplation is simplicity, which makes us see the face of God in everything, everyone, everywhere, all the time, and his hand in all the happenings; and makes us do all that we do — whether we think, study, work, speak, eat, or take our rest — under the loving gaze of the Father, being totally available to him in any form he may come to us.

What is contemplation? To live the life of Jesus. This is what I understand — to love Jesus, to live his life in us, to live our life in his life. That's contemplation. We must have a clean heart to be able to see: no jealousy, anger, contention, and especially no uncharitableness....

To me, contemplation is not to be shut up in a dark place but to allow Jesus to live his passion, love and humility in us, praying with us, being with us, sanctifying through us.

—HW, 33–35

If we neglect prayer and if the branch is not connected with the vine, it will die. That connecting of the branch to the vine is prayer. If that connection is there then love is there, then joy is there, and we will be the sunshine of God's love, the hope of eternal happiness, the flame of burning love. Why? Because we are one with Jesus.   —TS, 110

Spend your time in prayer. If you pray you will have faith, and if you have faith you will naturally want to serve. The one who prays cannot but have faith, and when you have faith you want to put it into action. Faith in action is service. Faith in action becomes a delight because it gives you the opportunity of putting your love for Christ into action — it is meeting Christ, serving Christ.   —TS, 112

You need especially to pray, for in our society, the work is only the fruit of prayer...our love in action. If you are really in love with Christ, no matter how small the work, it will be done better; it will be wholehearted. If your work is slapdash, then your love for God is slapdash. Your work must prove your love.
                                                —TS, 112

It is impossible to engage in the apostolate without being a soul of prayer, without a conscious awareness of and submission to the divine will. We must be aware of our oneness with Christ, as he was aware of his oneness with his Father. Our activity is truly apostolic only insofar as we permit him to work in and through us — with his power, his desire, his love. We must become holy, not because we want to *feel* holy, but because Christ must be able to live his life fully in us.   —TS, 113

The words of Jesus, "Love one another, even as I have loved you," should be not only a light to us, but they should also be a flame consuming the selfishness which prevents our growth in holiness. Jesus loved us to the end, "to the very limit of love, to the cross." This love must come from within — from our union with Christ. It must be an outpouring of our love for God. Loving must be as normal to us as living and breathing, day after day until our death. To understand this and practice it we need much prayer, the kind that unites us with God and overflows continually upon others. Our works of charity are nothing but the overflow of our love of God from within. Therefore, the one who is most united to him loves her neighbor most.

—TS, 114

The true interior life makes the active life burn forth and consume everything. It makes us find Jesus in the dark holes of the slums, in the most pitiful miseries of the poor — the God-Man naked on the cross, mournful, despised by all, the man of suffering crushed like a worm by the scourging and the crucifixion. This interior life motivates the Missionary of Charity to serve Jesus in the poor.   —TS, 117

Have I really learned to pray the work? Maybe I have never learned to pray the work because the whole time my mind is on "work." Here are words that will help you: "With Jesus, for Jesus, to Jesus." If you want to know how much you love Jesus, there is no need to ask anybody to tell you. In the sincerity of your heart you will know, if you practice silence.   —TS, 128

You have done a lot of work these days; it was nicely done, but did you give what was inside of you? What did that giving mean to you? Did you give with love and respect? If you did not pray that giving it was just a giving of self.

Did the people see you give with love and respect? Did you give the medicine with faith to the sick Christ? This is the difference between you and the social worker.   —TS, 128

It is not possible to engage in the direct apostolate without being a soul of prayer. We must be aware of oneness with Christ, as he was aware of oneness with his Father. Our activity is truly apostolic only insofar as we permit him to work in us and through us, with his power, with his desire, with his love. We must become holy, not because we want to feel holy, but because Christ must be able to live his life fully in us. We are to be all love, all faith, all purity, for the sake of the poor we serve. And when we have learned to seek God and his will, our contacts with the poor will become the means of great sanctity to ourselves and to others.   — SBG, 47

We must join our prayer with work. We try to bring this across to our sisters by inviting them to make their work a prayer. How is it possible to change one's work into a prayer? Work cannot substitute for prayer. Nevertheless, we can learn to make work a prayer. How can we do this? By doing our work with Jesus and for Jesus. That is the way to make our work a prayer. It is possible that I may not be able to keep my attention fully on God while I work, but God doesn't demand that I do so. Yet I can fully desire and intend that my work be done with Jesus and for Jesus. This is beautiful and that is what God wants. He wants our will and our desire to be for him, for our family, for our children, for our brethren, and for the poor.

The poor are a gift that God bestows on us. But they need our life of prayer and our oneness with God. Real prayer is union with God, a union as vital as that of the vine and the branches, which is the illustration Jesus gives us in the Gospel of John. We need prayer. We need that union to produce good fruit. The fruit is what we produce with our hands, whether it be food, clothing, money, or something else. All of that is the fruit of our oneness with God. We need a life of prayer, of poverty, and of sacrifice to do this with love.
                                    — OHFL, 58–59

We should not be afraid to give Jesus to others. We should not be afraid to put our love into action. We should not be afraid to pray, to work, and to make our work a prayer. This is what a distinguished person in India said, "When I see the

sisters in the streets of Calcutta, I always have the impression that Jesus Christ has come again into the world and that he is again going about, doing good works through the sisters." These words, expressed in such a beautiful way, are moving to me. I like to repeat them to everyone, especially to you, my co-workers. Through your deeds done to help the poor, Christ is going about doing good. Those who see us will see Christ in us.
— OHFL, 68

These two lives, action and contemplation, instead of excluding each other, call for each other's help, implement and complete each other. Action, to be productive, has need of contemplation. The latter, when it gets to a certain degree of intensity, diffuses some of its excess on the first. By contemplation the soul draws directly from the heart of God the graces which the active life must distribute.
— JWS, 8

The contemplative and apostolic fruitfulness of our way of life depends on our being rooted in Christ Jesus our Lord by our deliberate choice of small and simple means for the fulfillment of our mission and by our fidelity to humble work of love among the spiritually poorest, identifying ourselves with them, sharing their poverty and insecurities until it hurts.
— JWS, 23

Our active brothers and sisters put their service into action, and contemplative brothers and sisters put that loving action into prayer, into penance, into adoration, into contemplation, and into the proclamation of the word that they have meditated and adored. Active and contemplative are not two different lives; it is only that one is faith in action through service, the other faith in action through prayer.
— JWS, 66

Love — really be a contemplative in the heart of the world. Whatever you do, even if you help somebody cross the road, you do it to Jesus. Even giving somebody a glass of water, you

do it to Jesus. Such simple little teaching, but it is more and
more important.   —JWS, 73

The contemplative aspect of our missionary call makes us
gather the whole universe and bring it to the very center of
our heart, where he who is the source and the Lord of the
universe abides, and remain in communion with him, drinking
deeply from the very source the deep calm and peace of interior
quietude and refreshment of God, allowing the pure water of
divine grace to flow plentifully and unceasingly from the source
itself on to the whole of his creation.   —MTR, 22

3

A Loving Life

Mother Teresa was able to focus on God, and "pray" her work and daily life, because she was completely consumed by her love for Jesus in whatever form he chose to be manifested. She loved him especially in the poorest of the poor. She loved him in all human beings, her brothers and sisters, regardless of their origin, ethnicity, race, religion, gender, or any other difference, for "we are all children of God" (MTWL, 31), as she said. She insisted that love should begin at home, in the family. Love for every member of the family, the unborn included, is a basic factor for a peaceful society. Every family should live in love and peace like the Holy Family of Nazareth.

"THE REVOLUTION OF LOVE"

One cannot say, "Love God, not your neighbor." St. John calls liars those who pretend to love God but do not love their neighbor. How can we love the God whom we do not see if we do not love our fellow human being whom we do see? Whom we can touch? With whom we live? It is important to realize that love, to be genuine, must bring some suffering with it.

Jesus too suffered in order to love us. He still suffers. To be sure that we might remember his great love he became our

bread of life to satisfy our hunger for his love, our hunger for
God, because it was for this love that we were created. We were
created to love and to be loved, and he became man to enable
us to love him as he loves us. He has become one with the hungry, the naked, the homeless, the sick, the persecuted, the lonely,
the abandoned ones; and he tells us: "You made me like this."
He hungers for our love, and this is the hunger that afflicts our
poor people. This is the hunger that every one of us ought to
seek out. It might even be found in our own homes.

— MTLW, 137

It is very difficult, if not impossible, to give Jesus to others if we do
not already have him in our hearts.... To "convert" is to bring to
God. To "sanctify" is to fill with God. To convert and sanctify are
works of God. Our work is to love, to bear witness to God who
is love.... We do not try to impose our faith on others. We only
try to act in such a way that Christ will infuse his light and life
in us and, through us, into the world of suffering.... Nationality
means nothing in the rules of our Constitutions... and for that
reason we must never have an unfavorable attitude toward those
of another nationality or religion....

We must never be afraid to proclaim the good news in any envi-
ronment. I notice that people today have a greater hunger for God
than they did yesterday. Previously there was a great deal of external religiosity, but now there is in many persons a desire to find
God in the interior of the heart. This is the reason why especially
today we should be bearers and proclaimers of Christ....

In India we have an ever greater number of Hindus, Muslims,
Buddhists who take part in our work. Why do they come to us?
Because they sense the presence of God; they want to serve God
in their way, and they realize that with prayer and sacrifice they
can really do so.   — MTLL, 112

When we opened Baroda, a group of Hindus came to me and
said: "Have you come to convert us?" I looked at them, smiled,

and said: "Of course; this is the treasure that I have. I would be pleased if all of you became Christians voluntarily, but I do not have the power or the desire to force anyone. Not even God can force anyone who does not wish it...."

Goodness has converted more persons than zeal, knowledge or eloquence.... If we want the poor to see Christ in us, we must first see Christ in them. —MTLL, 111

It is through love of God and of neighbor that one arrives at complete happiness, at total service without limits, thus giving God to others, a God of peace, a living God, a God of love.
—MTLL, 48

The poor are a gift from God; they are who we love the most. Christ will not ask us how much we have done, but how much love we have put into our actions. Keep the light of Christ burning in your hearts. He alone is the way to follow. He is the truth that we must speak. He is the love that we must love....

Our work is simply an expression of our love of God. We should pour out our love, and others will be the means of expressing our love of God. I think that no one has given more than God, and he has given it all freely.... We should constantly thank God for giving us his Son Jesus, for he was born into the world like ourselves, and he was like us in all things except sin. God has manifested the grandeur and beauty of human life by becoming man. —MTLL, 49–50

All of us, you and I, should use what God has given us, that for which God created us. For God has created us for great things: to love and to give love.... That is why we are able to give Jesus to others.... People do not hunger for us, for our works, for our care. People hunger for God, for Jesus Christ, for the Eucharist.... This is love in action or active love. While on earth, we cannot see Jesus and therefore cannot even express our love for him. But every day we see and live through our

love. Every day we see and live with our neighbor, and therefore we can and should do what we would do for Christ if he
were visible. We should be available for God so he can use us.
Let us put love into practice, and then the hopes of the world
will not be in vain, futile, or frustrated, because through love
we find love, Jesus Christ.   —MTLL, 15

If we want to conquer the world, we cannot do it with bombs
or any other weapons of destruction. Let us conquer the world
with our love. Let us weave into our lives the links of the chain
of sacrifice and of love; then it will be possible for us to conquer
the world.   —MTLL, 91

Every time we let Jesus love others through us, it is Christmas.
                                                  —MTLL, 17

Let us pray that we may be able to welcome Jesus at Christmas,
not in the cold manger of our heart, but with a heart full of
love and humility, a heart warm with reciprocal love like that
of Mary.   —MTLL, 17

I cannot imagine a day without Jesus, because he is my life,
my love; he is everything to me. He came to give us the good
news that God loves us, that God is love, that he loves you
and me, and that we should love one another as he loves each
one of us.... When we look at the manger, we understand how
much he loves us through his suffering. When we contemplate
the cross, we understand how much he loved us: He died on the
cross because he loved us, and he wants us to love one another
as he loved us.   —MTLL, 18

We know that if we really want to love we must learn how to
forgive.   —GG, 34

There is always the danger that we may become only social
workers, or just do the work for the sake of the work. It is a

danger if we forget to whom we are doing it. Our works are
only an expression of our love for Christ. Our hearts need to
be full of love for him, and since we have to express that love
in action, naturally then the poorest of the poor are the means
of expressing our love for God.... A Hindu gentleman said that
they and we are doing social work, and the difference between
them and us is that they are doing it for something, and we are
doing it for Somebody.

This experience which we have by serving them, we must
pass on to people who have not had that beautiful experience.
It is one of the great rewards of our work.   —GG, 41–42

A smile must always be on our lips for any child to whom we
offer help, for any to whom we give companionship or medicine. It would be very wrong to offer only our cures; we must
offer to all our heart. Government agencies accomplish many
things in the field of assistance. We must offer something else:
Christ's love.   —GG, 44

"Thou shalt love the Lord thy God with thy whole heart,
with thy whole soul, and with thy whole mind." This is the
commandment of the great God, and he cannot command the
impossible. Love is a fruit in season at all times, and within
reach of every hand. Anyone may gather it and no limit is
set. Everyone can reach this love through meditation, spirit of
prayer, and sacrifice, by an intense inner life....

There is no limit, because God is love and love is God, and so
you are really in love with God. And then, God's love is infinite.
But part is to love and to give until it hurts. And that's why
it's not how much you do, but how much love you put into
the action. How much love we put in our presents. That's why
people — maybe they are very rich people — who have not got a
capacity to give and to receive love are the poorest of the poor.
And I think this is what our sisters have got — the spreading

of joy that you see in many religious people who have given themselves without reserve to God....

Our work is only the expression of the love we have for God. We have to pour our love on someone, and the people are the means of expressing our love for God.   —GG, 67–68

To show great love for God and our neighbor we need not do great things. It is how much love we put in the doing that makes our offering Something Beautiful for God.   —GG, 69

There is no great difference in reality between one country and another, because it is always people you meet everywhere. They may look different or be dressed differently, they may have a different education or position; but they are all the same. They are all people to be loved; they are all hungry for love.
                                                        —GG, 53

In England and other places, in Calcutta, in Melbourne, in New York, we find lonely people who are known by the number of their room. Why are we not there? Do we really know that there are some people, maybe next-door to us? Maybe there is a blind man who would be happy if you would read the newspaper for him; maybe there is a rich person who has no one to visit him — he has plenty of other things, he is nearly drowned in them, but there is not that touch and he needs your touch. Some time back a very rich man came to our place, and he said to me: "Please, either you or somebody, come to my house. I am nearly half-blind and my wife is nearly mental; our children have all gone abroad, and we are dying of loneliness, we are longing for the loving sound of a human voice."

Let us not be satisfied with just giving money. Money is not enough, money can be got, but they need your hearts to love them. So, spread love everywhere you go: first of all in your home. Give love to your children, to your wife or husband, to a next-door neighbor.   —GG, 64–65

A Christian is a tabernacle of the living God. He created me, he chose me, he came to dwell in me, because he wanted me. Now that you have known how much God is in love with you, it is but natural that you spend the rest of your life radiating that love....

To be a true Christian means the true acceptance of Christ, and the becoming of another Christ one to another. To love as we are loved, and as Christ has loved us from the cross, we have to love each other and give to others....

When Christ said: "I was hungry and you fed me," he didn't mean only the hunger for bread and for food; he also meant the hunger to be loved. Jesus himself experienced this loneliness. He came among his own and his own received him not, and it hurt him then and it has kept on hurting him. The same hunger, the same loneliness, the same having no one to be accepted by and to be loved and wanted by. Every human being in that case resembles Christ in his loneliness; and that is the hardest part, that's real hunger.   —GG, 30–31

There is hunger for ordinary bread, and there is hunger for love, for kindness, for thoughtfulness; and this is the great poverty that makes people suffer so much.   —GG, 19–20

The words of Jesus, "Love one another as I have loved you," must be not only a light for us but a flame that consumes the self in us. Love, in order to survive, must be nourished by sacrifices, especially the sacrifice of self.

Suffering is nothing by itself. But suffering shared with the passion of Christ is a wonderful gift, the most beautiful gift, a token of love....

I must be willing to give whatever it takes to do good to others. This requires that I be willing to give until it hurts. Otherwise, there is no true love in me and I bring injustice, not peace, to those around me.   —HW, 48–49

One day I visited a house where our sisters shelter the aged. This is one of the nicest houses in England, filled with beautiful and precious things, yet there was not one smile on the faces of these people. All of them were looking toward the door.

I asked the sister in charge, "Why are they like that? Why can't you see a smile on their faces?" (I am accustomed to seeing smiles on people's faces. I think a smile generates a smile, just as love generates love.)

The sister answered, "The same thing happens every day. They are always waiting for someone to come and visit them. Loneliness eats them up, and day after day they do not stop looking. Nobody comes."

Abandonment is an awful poverty. There are poor people everywhere, but the deepest poverty is not being loved.

The poor we seek may live near us or far away. They can be materially or spiritually poor. They may be hungry for bread or hungry for friendship. They may need clothing, or they may need the sense of wealth that God's love for them represents. They may need the shelter of a house made of bricks and cement or the shelter of having a place in our hearts.

—HW, 65–66

I never look at the masses as my responsibility. I look at the individual. I can love only one person at a time. I can feed only one person at a time. Just one, one, one.

You get closer to Christ by coming closer to each other. As Jesus said, "Whatever you do to the least of my brethren, you do to me." So you begin...I begin. I picked up one person — maybe if I didn't pick up that one person I wouldn't have picked up 42,000.

The whole work is only a drop in the ocean. But if I didn't put the drop in, the ocean would be one drop less.

Same thing for you, same thing in your family, same thing in the church where you go. Just begin...one, one, one.

—WLB, 79

Let us not be satisfied with just giving money; money is not enough, for money one can get. The poor need our hands to serve them, they need our hearts to love them. The religion of Christ is love, the spreading of love....

I try to give to the poor people for love what the rich could get for money. No, I wouldn't touch a leper for a thousand pounds; yet I willingly cure him for the love of God.
—GG, 51–52

At the time of death, when we meet God face-to-face, we will be judged concerning love, concerning how much we have loved. Not concerning how much we have accomplished, but rather how much love we have put into what we have done.

In order for love to be genuine, it has to be above all a love for my neighbor. Love for my neighbor will lead me to true love for God. What the sisters, the brothers, and the co-workers try to do all over the world is to put into loving action their love for God.
—HJ, 114–15

The aim of the Missionaries of Charity is to take God, to take his love, to the homes of the poor and thus to lead them to him. It does not matter who they are, nor what their nationality or social status may be. We intend to make them understand the love and compassion that God has for them, which is a love of predilection.
—HJ, 119–20

It is easy to love those who live far away. It is not always easy to love those who live right next to us. It is easier to offer a dish of rice to meet the hunger of a needy person than to comfort the loneliness and the anguish of someone in our own home who does not feel loved.
—HJ, 120

"Love one another." Suppress this command, and the whole work of the church of Christ will fall.

Charity toward the poor must be a burning flame in our society. Just as the fire, when it ceases burning, spreads no more
warmth, so the Missionaries of Charity, should they lack love,
would lose all usefulness and would have no more life.

Charity is like a living flame: the drier the fuel, the livelier
the flame. Likewise our hearts, when they are free of all earthly
causes, commit themselves in free service.

Love of God must give rise to a total service. The more dis-
gusting the work is, the greater must love be, as it takes succor
to the Lord disguised in the rags of the poor.   —HJ, 130

People are hungry for God. People are hungry for love. Are you
aware of that? Do you know that? Do you see that? Do you
have eyes to see? Quite often we look but we don't see. We
are all passing through this world. We need to open our eyes
and see.

You have received a lot from your brethren: the gift of love.
You have seen love in action through their lives. Take their
example to heart, the example of sacrificial giving. Before anything else look for the poor in your own homes and on the
street where you live. There are lonely people around you in
hospitals and psychiatric wards. There are so many people that
are homeless!

In New York, our sisters are working among the destitute
who are dying. What pain it causes to see these people! They are
only known by their street address now. Yet they were all someone's children. Someone loved them at one time. They loved
others during their lifetime. But now they are only known by
their street address.   —OHFL, 11

Let's believe in God's love, and let's be faithful to him. If you
look at the cross, you will see his head lowered to kiss you. You
will see his arms stretched out to embrace you. You will see his
heart open to welcome you. Don't be afraid. He loves us, and he
wants us to love one another. He loves us in spite of how poor

and sinful we are. His love is true, and we should believe in his love. If we truly believe, it will not be hard for us to identify with the poor, even the poor in our own homes.

—OHFL, 44–45

When a girl who belongs to a very old caste comes to place herself at the service of the outcasts, we are talking about a revolution, the biggest one, the hardest of all: the revolution of love!   —MLP, 12

"ANY TASK OF LOVE IS A TASK OF PEACE"

Everybody today seems to be in a hurry. No one has any time to give to others: children to their parents, parents to their children, spouses to each other.

World peace begins to break down in the homes.

—OW, 50

Today countries are concentrating too much on efforts and means to defend their borders. Yet these countries know so little about the poverty and suffering that make the human beings who live inside such borders feel so lonely!

If instead they would worry about giving these defenseless beings some food, some shelter, some healthcare, some clothes, it is undeniable that the world would be a more peaceful and happy place to live.   —OW, 34

We shall make this year a year of Peace in a particular way — to be able to do this we shall try to talk more to God and with God and less with men and to men. Let us preach the peace of Christ like he did. He went about doing good; he did not stop his works of charity because the Pharisees and others hated him or tried to spoil his Father's work. He just went about doing good. Cardinal Newman wrote: "Help me to spread the fragrance everywhere I go — let me preach thee without preaching, not by words but by my example — by the catching force; the sympathetic influence of what I do, the evident fullness of the love my heart bears to thee." Our works of love are nothing but works of peace. Let us do them with greater love and efficiency — each in her own or his own work in daily life; in your home — in your neighbor. It is always the same Christ who says:

I was hungry — not only for food, but for peace that comes from a pure heart.

I was thirsty — not for water, but for peace that satiates the passionate thirst of passion for war.

I was naked — not for a shelter made of bricks, but for a heart that understands, that covers, that loves. This year let us be this to Christ in our neighbor wherever the Missionaries of Charity and their co-workers be. Let us radiate the peace of God and so light his light and extinguish in the world and in the hearts of all men all hatred, and love for power. Let the Missionaries of Charity and the co-workers, in every country wherever they are, meet God with a smile — everywhere they go in everyone.   — SBG, 52

Co-workers should give love in action. Our works of love are nothing but works of peace. Let us do them with greater love and efficiency, each in his or her own work, in daily life, at home, with one's neighbor.   — GG, 38

54A, A.J.C. Bose Road,
Calcutta — 16
2nd January, 1991

Dear President George Bush and President Saddam Hussein:
    I come to you with tears in my eyes and God's love in my heart to plead to you for the poor and those who will become

poor if the war that we all dread and fear happens. I beg you
with my whole heart to work for, to labor for God's peace and
to be reconciled with one another.

You both have your cases to make and your people to care
for, but first please listen to the One who came into the world
to teach us peace. You have the power and the strength to destroy God's presence and image, his men, his women, and his
children. Please listen to the will of God. God has created us to
be loved by his love and not to be destroyed by our hatred.

In the short term there may be winners and losers in this war
that we all dread but that never can and never will justify the
suffering, pain and loss of life which your weapons will cause.

I come to you in the name of God, the God that we all love
and share, to beg for the innocent ones, our poor of the world
and those who will become poor because of war. They are the
ones who will suffer and when they do we will be the ones who
are guilty for not having done all in our power to protect and
love them. I plead to you for those who will be left orphaned,
widowed, and left alone because their parents, husbands, brothers and children have been killed. *I beg you please save them.*
I plead for those who will be left with disability and disfigure-
ment. They are God's children. I plead for those who will be
left with no home, no food, and no love. Please think of them
as being your children. Finally I plead for those who will have
the most precious thing that God can give us, Life, taken away
from them. I beg you to save our brothers and sisters, yours
and ours, because they are given to us by God to love and to
cherish. It is not for us to destroy what God has given to us.
Please, please let your mind and your will become the mind and
will of God. You have the power to bring war into the world
or to build peace. Please choose the way of peace. I, my sisters,
and our poor are praying for you so much. The whole world
is praying that you will open your hearts in love to God. You
may win the war but what will the cost be on people who are
broken, disabled, and lost?

I appeal to you — to your love, your love of God and your
fellowmen. In the name of God and in the name of those you
will make poor do not destroy life and peace. Let the love and
peace triumph and let your name be remembered for the good
you have done, the joy you have spread, and the love you have
shared.

Please pray for me and my sisters as we try to love and serve
the poor because they belong to God and are loved in his eyes
so we and our poor are praying for you. We pray that you
will love and nourish what God has so lovingly entrusted into
your care.

May God bless you now and always.

— MTB, 225–27

The same loving hand that has created you has created me. If he
is your Father, he must be my Father also. We all belong to the
same family. Hindus, Muslims, and all peoples are our brothers
and sisters. They too are the children of God.

Our work among the Hindus proclaims that God loves them,
God has created them, they are my brothers and sisters. Naturally I would like to give them the joy of what I believe, but that
I cannot do; only God can. Faith is a gift of God, but God does
not force himself.

Christians, Muslims, Hindus, believers, and nonbelievers have
the opportunity with us to do works of love, have the opportunity
with us to share the joy of loving and come to realize God's
presence. Hindus become better Hindus. Catholics become better
Catholics. Muslims become better Muslims.

— WLB, 35

All human beings are brothers and sisters. All of us have been
created by the same loving hand of God. Jesus has said to us all,
"Love one another as I have loved you" (John 15:12). And he
has also said, "As the Father has loved me, so love one another"
(see John 15:9).

Having this command of Jesus, we cannot be known for a partisan spirit.   —HJ, 113

No one should avoid the smallest tasks. Any task of love is a task of peace, no matter how insignificant it may seem.

In the world there is too much hatred, too much fighting. We will not be able to put them away with guns or bombs or any kind of weapon that wounds. We will attain that only through gestures of love, joy, and peace.   —HJ, 121

In our work we can be attracted to idle chatter. Let us be attentive not to run this danger when we visit families. We can fall into talking about this and that, forgetting the central point of our visit.

We want to and we must take the peace of Christ: let us not be vehicles of dissension. We must never consent to anybody talking to us against his neighbors.

If we run across a family who are in a bad mood and who are prone to slide into topics that are contrary to charity, let us slip in some words to make them think a little about God. Then let us go away, for no good is possible if the nerves are excited.

We must do the same with those who make us lose precious time. If the search for God does not attract them, let us leave them. We have no time to lose.   —HJ, 132

I think that abortion is the greatest destroyer of peace today precisely because it is war. It is killing. It is a deliberate and calculated murder carried out with the mother's collaboration. We read in Scripture what God clearly says about this: "Even if a mother should forget her child, I shall not forsake you. You are in the palm of my hand." God has us in the very palm of his hand. And that is what strikes me. Even if a mother could forget her child, which seems impossible, "I will not forsake you." Today abortion is the greatest and most effective destroyer of peace.   —OHFL, 80

I think there is something that can make us live joyfully. It is that Jesus is with us. He loves us. If each one of us would simply remember that God loves us and is giving us the chance to love others in that love — not so much in big things but in the little things of life — our countries could become full of God's love. And how beautiful it would be if the power of peace would go forth and destroy the power to make war and take life. How great it would be to see the joy of life break forth into the lives of the unborn! If you become this kind of torch lit for peace in the world, then indeed the Nobel Peace Prize will be a true gift from the Norwegian people.   — OHFL, 88

As Jesus' co-workers, one thing we have to learn is to sow joy. We don't need bombs or weapons to bring peace to the world. We need that love and compassion that we ask for every day. We need a truly compassionate love — a compassion and love that bring joy and peace. The world is hungry for God.
                                               — OHFL, 90–91

By following the vocation of a Missionary of Charity, we stand before the world as ambassadors of peace by preaching the message of love in action that crosses all barriers of nationality, creed, or country.

The Indian ambassador in Rome told the people, "These our sisters have done more in a short time to bring our two countries closer to each other by their influence of love than we have through official means."   — JWS, 89–90

All of us should work for peace. But to obtain that peace all of us have to learn from Jesus to be meek and humble of heart. Only humility will lead us to unity, and unity to peace. To that end, let us help each other draw closer to Jesus, so that we may learn the lesson of humility with joy.   — MTR, 58

Lord, make us worthy to serve men, our brothers, who are dispersed all over the world, who live and die in poverty and hunger. Give to all of them, through our hands, their daily bread, and through our understanding love give them peace and joy.   —MTR, 166

Love is not something that fossilizes, but something that lives. Works of love are the way to peace. And where does this love begin? — right in our hearts. We must know that we have been created for greater things, not just to be a number in the world, not just to go for diplomas and degrees, this work and that work. We have been created in order to love and to be loved.

—MTR, 257

To make it easy for you and for me to see Jesus, he made himself the Bread of Life, so that we can receive life, so that we may have a life of peace, a life of joy. Find Jesus, and you will find peace.   —MTR, 162

In order to spread joy, joy needs to reign in the family. Peace and war start within one's own home. If we really want peace for the world, let us start by loving one another within our families. We will thus have Christ's joy, which is our strength. Sometimes it is hard for us to smile at one another. It is often difficult for the husband to smile at his wife or for the wife to smile at her husband.   —MTR, 73

"LOVE BEGINS AT HOME"

In Jesus, Mary, and Joseph — the Holy Family of Nazareth — we have a beautiful example for us to imitate. What did they do?

Joseph was a humble carpenter in order to support Jesus and Mary, providing their food and clothes — whatever they needed.

Mary, the mother, also had a humble task — that of a housewife with a son and a husband to take care of.

As the son was growing up, Mary would worry that he would have a normal life, that he would "feel at home" in the house with her and with Joseph.

It was a home where tenderness, understanding, and mutual respect abounded.

As I said before: a wonderful example for us to imitate.

— OW, 50

I was amazed when I learned that in the West so many young are on drugs. I tried to understand the reason for this. Why? The answer is, "because in the family there is nobody who cares about them." Fathers and mothers are so busy they have no time. Young parents work, and the child lives in the street, and goes his own way. We speak of peace. These are the things that threaten peace. I think that today peace is threatened by abortion too, which is a true war, the direct killing of the child by its own mother. In the Bible we read that God clearly said: "Even though a mother did forget her infant, I will not forget him."

Today, abortion is the worst evil, and the greatest enemy of peace. We who are here today were wanted by our parents. We would not be here if our parents had not wanted us.

We want children, and we love them. But what about the other millions? Many are concerned about the children, like those in Africa, who die in great numbers either from hunger or for others reasons. But millions of children die intentionally, by the will of their mothers. This is what is destroying peace today. Because if a mother can kill her own child, what will prevent us from killing ourselves, or one another? Nothing.

— MTLW, 138

If there is so much suffering and sadness in the world today, it is because the child, the unborn child, the innocent child is unwanted, rejected, neglected.... A child is God's greatest gift to the family, to the nation, to the world. The child is a life from

God, created in the image of God, created for great things: to
love and be loved.   —MTLL, 30

Abortion is the greatest danger to peace. I believe that no
human hand should ever be raised to kill life. Every life is God's
life within us. Even the unborn child has God's life within itself.
We have no right to destroy this life, whatever the means we
use to do so.... An infant is always a gift from God....
    In my opinion, if abortion is permitted in wealthy countries
that have all the means that money can buy, those countries are
the poorest among the poor.... So many infants today are in
the category of the unwanted, the unloved.... It is a wonderful
thing when an infant has been able to escape death at the hands
of parents who have welcomed it.... This is one of the most
admirable characteristics of our people, namely, their willingness to adopt and to offer a home and love to these unwanted
babies; to Christ in the likeness of the infants.   —MTLL, 31

It is a noteworthy thing that God should have chosen an unborn
baby to give witness to him before the birth of Jesus, but it is
sad to think of all the infants that are unborn today through
the choice of their parents.... Abortion is the greatest danger
to peace, because we are able to destroy the life that is given by
God. If a mother can become the murderer of her children, what
can we say about other kinds of murders and wars in the world?
People today no longer love one another, and it is precisely here
that the danger to peace lies. Abortion is a source of evil in
the world.   —MTLL, 32

Life is a gift that God has given us. That life is present even in
the unborn.
    A human hand should never end a life.
    I am convinced that the screams of the children whose lives
have been terminated before their birth reach God's ears.
                                                        —OW, 67

I think the world today is upside-down, and is suffering so much, because there is so very little love in the homes and in family life. We have no time for our children, we have no time for each other; there is no time to enjoy each other. If we could only bring back into our lives the life that Jesus, Mary, and Joseph lived in Nazareth, if we could make our homes another Nazareth, I think that peace and joy would reign in the world....

Love begins at home; love lives in homes, and that is why there is so much suffering and so much unhappiness in the world today. If we listen to Jesus he will tell us what he said before: "Love one another, as I have loved you." He has loved us through suffering, dying on the cross for us, and so if we are to love one another, if we are to bring that love into life again, we have to begin at home....

We must make our homes centers of compassion and forgive endlessly....

Everybody today seems to be in such a terrible rush, anxious for greater developments and greater riches and so on, so that children have very little time for their parents. Parents have very little time for each other, and in the home begins the disruption of the peace of the world....

People who love each other fully and truly — they are the happiest people in the world, and we see that with our very poor people. They love their children, and they love their home. They may have very little, they may have nothing, but they are happy people....

A living love hurts. Jesus, to prove his love for us, died on the cross. The mother, to give birth to her child, has to suffer. If you really love one another properly, there must be sacrifice.

—GG, 11–13

The best and surest way to learn the love of Jesus is through the family.   —WLB, 50

We are created in the image of God, in the image of Jesus as a human being. Every child has been created for a greater thing — to love and be loved.

From the very beginning, from the time there is life, from the time there is conception, there is the life of God — the life of the living God.

That is why it is so wrong to destroy life — to destroy the image of God.   —WLB, 51

Many of the troubles of modern society are caused by broken families. Many mothers and fathers are so busy that they are never home.

Children come home from school and there is no one to receive them, to pay attention to them, to encourage them if they are sad, to share their joy if they are happy.

Children long for somebody to accept them, to love them, to praise them, to be proud of them.

If they do not have this, they will go to the streets where there are plenty of people ready to accept them. The child can be lost. Much hatred and destruction is caused when a child is lost to the family.

Like our Lady and St. Joseph we must go and search for the child. When Jesus was lost they went and searched. They did not sit and wait. They did not rest until they found him

We must bring the child back, make the child feel wanted. Without the child there is not hope.   —WLB, 53

Love begins at home. If we do not love one another whom we see twenty-four hours, how can we love those we see only once?

We show love by thoughtfulness, by kindness, by sharing joy, by sharing a smile.... Through the little things.

A little child has no difficulty in loving, has no obstacles to love. And that is why Jesus said, "Unless you become like little children...."   —WLB, 54

It is very important for children to hear their parents talk about God. The children must be able to ask about God.

Once I gave a prayer to a communist, and he took it back to his family and the children started to pray.

When he saw me again he said, "Mother, you don't know how your prayer and picture have disturbed the whole family. The children want to know who God is. They want to know why Mother is speaking this way."

The children are hungry. That is why we need to pray together. If the parent sets the example, the children will not forget how to pray, how they love each other, how they share sorrow, how they share joy.

Children watch...they watch and they grow with that.

They will learn that it makes a difference how they live their lives by watching what the parents do.   —WLB, 56

If we can bring prayer into the family, the family will stay together. They will love one another. Just get together for five minutes.

Start with the Our Father, that's all! Or we can say: "My Lord, I love you; my God, I am sorry; my God, I believe in you; my God, I trust you. Help us to love one another as you love us."

That is where your strength will come from when you teach each other in prayer.   —WLB, 57

Many of our children are unwanted and unloved. They need someone to care. The problem that worries so many people today is not the fact that the world is beginning to be over-populated. What we are beginning to see more and more is that there are people who are trying to prove that God's providence cannot provide for all the children yet to be born. In my opinion, if abortion is allowed in the rich countries that have everything that money can buy, then those countries are the poorest among the poor.   —OHFL, 31–32

Dear God of Joy,

Give me the grace to make my home another Nazareth where peace, love, and happiness reign. Let me love you through the love that is given to my family.

Let my mission of love begin in my own home, and then spread out to all who are in need of your love and grace. Let your love take root first in my heart and then in the hearts of all those with whom I come into contact.

Let my home be a center of kindness, compassion, and mercy. Give me the grace to make anyone who comes into contact with me go away better and happier.

Let the love I have given others, even in small ways, come back to me as your grace. Let me forgive always and grant that this forgiveness will return to me and flourish.

Let me begin then in the place where I am, with the people I know, and let the lamp of your love always shine in the windows of my heart and my home. Amen.   —APMT, 77

Where does that love begin? In our families. And how does it begin? By praying together. The family that prays together, stays together. And if you stay together, you will love one another as Jesus loves each person in your family.

—LJ, 13–14

We should never forget: love begins at home. Yes today, we are having a terrible time, because we have so many broken, unhappy families.

They don't pray together. There is no sharing. There is no joy of serving each other.

Poverty is not the cause.

No, it is not poverty.

What then is causing this?

It is unbridled ambition for things and for status, something that interferes in our lives, that we love more than our family.

That's why I very often tell young people, "It is very beautiful for a young man to love a young woman. And for a young woman to love a young man. But make sure you love each other with a pure heart, with a clean heart — more than money, more than any possession. The greatest gift you can give to each other is a clean heart and a virgin body." The loss of purity, of chastity, of virginity has affected so many lives.

I never tire of talking about family life and of expressing my desire for families to be holy and united, where love reigns among all family members.

How will husband and wife stay together? We have the marvelous example of the Holy Family of Nazareth in plain view.

Why do we call them the "Holy Family of Nazareth"? Because there was such living holiness among them. They were of one heart, full of love, in the very heart of God.

There was no division.

There was no misunderstanding.

We know how much St. Joseph loved Mary. When he found out that she was with child, he could have presumed the worst. He could have gone straight to the chief priest to denounce her for adultery. But no, he did not do it, because he loved her so tenderly! He would have preferred to be stoned rather than have Mary stoned. Here we have an example of tender love, of mutual concern. And an Angel told St. Joseph in a dream that this child was God's very own.

If father and mother have that concern for each other, naturally, the children will learn from them. And when the time comes for them to be parents, they will know what to do and how to do it.

Teach your children to love one another.

Teach your children to have respect for each other.

Teach your children to share.

Teach your children, because nowadays, many schools do not teach these things.

I will never forget how a little four-year-old Hindu child taught me how to show great love.

It was a time when we had no sugar in Calcutta. I do not know how that little one heard that Mother Teresa had no sugar for her children. He went home to his parents and told them, "I will not eat sugar for three days. I'll give my sugar to Mother Teresa."

That little one loved with great love. He loved until it hurt. And so must we.   —LJ, 80–82

Jesus was sent to bring us the good news that God is love, that he loves us. He wants us to love one another as he loves us.

Jesus was born into a family and stayed in Nazareth for thirty years.

He had come to redeem the world, yet he spent thirty years in Nazareth, doing the humble work of an ordinary person.

People often used to say, "But he is the son of Joseph! How could he do this . . . ? He is the son of Mary, we know him. . . . "

He spent all those years just living our family life.

They must have prayed together.

They must have worked together.

They must have loved each other.

Yes, that was true family life.

There was peace!

There was unity!

There was joy!

Bring prayer back into your family life, and you too will see that unity, the bond of joyful love that will bind you together. Maybe there is poverty and suffering in your families. But sharing together, loving together will help you.

—LJ, 107–8

All over the world, there is terrible suffering, terrible hunger for love. So bring prayer in your family, bring it to your little children. Teach them to pray. For a child that prays is a happy child. A family that prays is a united family. We hear of so many broken families. And then we examine them: why are they broken? I think because they never pray together. They are never one in prayer before the Lord.   —JWS, 52

My prayer for all families is that you grow in holiness through this love for each other. Bring Jesus wherever you go. Let them look up and see only Jesus in you. Pray for your children and pray that your daughters and sons will have the courage to say yes to God and to consecrate their lives totally to him. There are many, many families that would be so happy if their children would give their lives to God. So pray for them that they will be able to fulfill the heart's desire.   —JWS, 95

I always say — and I don't get tired of repeating it — that love starts at home. I will never forget that I was in a country once where there were many co-workers, but two of the coordinators for the co-workers were very distant from each other. And they were husband and wife. They came to me and I told them, "I can't understand how you are able to give Jesus to others if you can't give him to each other. How can you find Jesus hidden under the distressing appearance of the poor if you cannot see him in each other?"

The husband and wife started up an endless argument. Both of them let out all their frustrations and hurts, saying everything they had to say. Then I interrupted. "Now that's enough. You have said everything that you needed to say. Let's go to Jesus so that you can tell him all these things."

We went to the chapel and the two knelt down before the altar. After a few moments, the husband turned to his wife and said, "You are my only love in this world, the only one I love and have." Other things of that sort followed. It was all very beautiful.

Now all the co-workers there have changed for the better. Why? Because those in charge of the group have come to understand that if we don't accept Jesus in one another, we will not be able to give him to others.   —MTR, 252–53

I cannot forget my mother. She was usually very busy all day long. But when sunset drew near, it was her custom to hurry with her tasks in order to be ready to receive my father.

At the time we did not understand, and we would smile and even joke a little about it. Today I cannot help but call to mind that great delicacy of love that she had for him. No matter what happened, she was always prepared, with a smile on her lips, to welcome him.

Today we have no time. Fathers and mothers are so busy that when children come home they are not welcomed with love or with a smile. — MTR, 252

People are afraid of having children

Children have lost their place in the family.

Children are very lonely, very lonely!

When children come home from school, there is no one to greet them. Then they go back to the streets.

We must find our children again and bring them back home.

Mothers are at the heart of the family. Children need their mothers. If the mother is there, the children will be there too. For the family to be whole, the children and the mother also need the father to be present in the home.

I think if we can help to bring them all back together, we will do a beautiful thing for God. — MTR, 246

4

A Joyful Life

Mother Teresa showed the path to a joyful life through her love of God and neighbors. She loved especially the poorest of the poor. She chose to be poor herself following the steps of her Master. In serving the poor with love and dedication, she depended totally on divine providence and was never worried about the future. This kind of poverty was, for her, freedom and joy, which was one of the most effective ways for preaching the Gospel. But, to be able to do so, she realized that her life must be linked to Holy Communion. She could not imagine one single day without being in union with Christ in the Eucharist.

HOLY COMMUNION

In Holy Communion we have Christ under the appearance of bread. In our work we find him under the appearance of flesh and blood. It is the same Christ. "I was hungry, I was naked, I was sick, I was homeless." —SBG, 53

The Mass is the spiritual food that sustains me. I could not pass a single day or hour in my life without it. In the Eucharist, I see Christ in the appearance of bread. In the slums, I see Christ in the distressing disguise of the poor — in the broken bodies, in the children, in the dying. That is why this work becomes possible. — MTB, 209–10

I cannot imagine being without the Eucharist for even a day.... Nourished by his love, I touch him, love him, and serve him in the poor.... The life of him who has become the Bread of Life is the selfsame life of him who is dying on the street and is in need of our help, the selfsame life of the unborn infant.
— MTLL, 54

Our lives must be constantly nourished by the Eucharist. Because if we are unable to see Christ under the appearance of bread, neither shall we discover him under the humble appearance of the emaciated bodies of the poor....

Faith in act is love, and love in act is service. Jesus said: "I was hungry, I was naked, I was homeless.... You have done this to me." We take Christ at his word, and we believe in him. For this reason we have need of the Eucharist, because he has become the bread of life to satisfy our desires, our needs, and our love for him. These are the reasons why our life must be closely linked to the Eucharist....

Jesus became the bread of life so that you and I could eat and live. The meaning of the Eucharist is comprehensive love. Jesus understands; he understands that we have a terrible hunger for God. He understood that we were created for love. That is why he became the bread of life.... The tabernacle is the proof that he has made his dwelling among us for ever.
— MTLL, 55

"Because the loaf of bread is one, we, many though we are, are one body, for we all partake of the one loaf" (1 Cor. 10:17). Today we also come together for community gatherings, for daily and weekly meetings, and especially on Sundays for the celebration of the Eucharist, the mystery of our faith. There we proclaim the death and resurrection of Christ; we are nourished by his presence and love; we pray together.

My great love is Jesus in the Eucharist, in Holy Communion. There I meet him, I receive him, I love him; then I rediscover him and serve him in the poorest of the poor. Without daily Communion my life would be empty, useless; my work would be superfluous.... Only with assiduous prayer and with Communion are we able to live with Jesus and for Jesus with our poor and for our poor and needy.   — MTLL, 93

Look at the tabernacle.... Note the meaning of this love. Ask yourself: Do I understand this? Is my heart so pure that I can see Jesus within it? Find Jesus and you will find peace. The time that we spend in daily dialogue with God is the most precious part of our whole day.   — MTLL, 119

In our hearts let us adore Jesus, who spent thirty of his thirty-three years in silence and began his public life with forty days of silence.... Let us adore Jesus in the silence of the Eucharist. ...People do not hunger for us. They hunger for God. They hunger for Jesus in the Eucharist. He gives us himself in the Eucharist and invites us to grow in his love. Christ's love for us gives us strength and prompts us to give ourselves for him.... In this way we make Jesus present in the world today. We cannot separate our life from the Eucharist.... People ask: "Where do the sisters get the joy and energy to do all that they do?" The Eucharist should be at the center of our life. Ask Jesus to remain with you, to work with you, so that you can transform your work into prayer.... The Eucharist is so small, but it produces great effects, because it is the bread of life and of love. Without Jesus I would not be able to live my life for a single day or a single hour.   — MTLL, 121

If we truly understand the Eucharist; if we make the Eucharist the central focus of our lives; if we feed our lives with the Eucharist, we will not find it difficult to discover Christ, to love him, and to serve him in the poor....

The Eucharist is something more than simply receiving Christ. It supposes that we satisfy his hunger.

Christ invites us, "Come to me."

Christ hungers for souls.

Nowhere in the Gospel has Christ ever uttered an expression of rejection.

Rather, we always find an invitation: "Come to me."

—OW, 97

Christ changed himself into bread of life. Changing himself into bread, he became totally at our disposal so that, having been fed by him, we would feel the strength necessary to give ourselves to others. —OW, 100

We need the Eucharist because Jesus has become the bread of life in order to meet our desires, our longings, our love for him. This is why our life needs to be closely linked to the Eucharist. We begin our day with the Holy Mass and Communion, and we finish the day with an hour of adoration, which unites us with Jesus and with the poor in whom we offer our services.

—HJ, 123

To live out such a calling every Missionary of Charity must have a life focused on the Eucharist. We see Christ in the Eucharist under the appearance of bread, while we see him in the poor under the distressing disguise of poverty. The Eucharist and the poor are nothing more than the same love of God. To be able to see and love Jesus in the poor, we must be one with Christ through a life of deep prayer. That is why the sisters start their day with Mass and meditation. And they finish it with adoration of the Blessed Sacrament. Communion with Christ gives us our strength, our joy, and our love. —OHFL, 27

Where will you get the joy of loving? — in the Eucharist, Holy
Communion. Jesus has made himself the bread of life to give
us life. Night and day, he is there. If you really want to grow
in love, come back to the Eucharist, come back to that adoration. In our congregation, we used to have adoration once
a week for one hour, and then in 1973, we decided to have
adoration one hour every day. We have much work to do. Our
homes for the sick and dying destitute are full everywhere. And
from the time we started having adoration every day, our love
for Jesus became more intimate, our love for each other more
understanding, our love for the poor more compassionate, and
we have double the number of vocations. God has blessed us
with many wonderful vocations.   —JWS, 62–63

Look at the tabernacle — see how much this love means now.
Do I know that? Is my heart so clean that I can see Jesus there?
And to make it easy for you and for me to see Jesus, he made
himself the bread of life, so that we can receive life, so that we
may have a life of peace, a life of joy. Find Jesus, and you will
find peace.   —JWS, 63

We shall spend two hours a day at sunrise and sunset in adoration of Jesus in the Blessed Sacrament exposed. Our hours
of adoration will be special hours of reparation for sins and
intercession for the needs of the whole world, exposing the
sin-sick and suffering humanity to the healing, sustaining, and
transforming rays of Jesus, radiating from the Eucharist.
                                                   —MTR, 168

The Eucharist is the sacrament of prayer, the fountain and sum-
mit of Christian life. Our Eucharist is incomplete if it does not
lead us to service and love for the poor. As we receive the
communion of the poor, we discover our own poverty....
     Our life is linked to the Eucharist. Through faith in and love
of the body of Christ under the appearance of bread, we take

Christ literally: "I was hungry and you gave me food. I was a stranger and you welcomed me, naked and you clothed me. . . . "

Put your sins in the chalice for the Precious Blood to wash away. One drop is capable of washing away all the sins of the world.   — MTR, 178

The Eucharist involves more than just receiving; it also involves satisfying the hunger of Christ. He says, "Come to me." He is hungry for souls. Nowhere does the Gospel say: "Go away," but always "Come to me."

Our lives must be woven around the Eucharist. Ask Jesus to be with you, to work with you that you may be able to pray the work. You must really be sure that you have received Jesus. After that, you cannot give your tongue, your thoughts, or your heart to bitterness.   — MTR, 180

Christ made himself the Bread of Life. He wanted to give himself to us in a very special way — in a simple, tangible way — because it is hard for human beings to love God whom they cannot see. . . .   — MTR, 185

When we remember that every morning at Communion we have held in our hands all the holiness of God, we feel more willing to abstain from everything that may stain our purity. Thence flows a sincere and deep respect for our own person — respect also toward others leading us to treat them with sensitivity but likewise abstaining from all disordered sentimentality.
                                                            — MTR, 185

Holy Communion, as the word itself implies, is the intimate union of Jesus and our soul and body. If we want to have life and have it more abundantly, we must live on the flesh of our Lord. The saints understood so well that they could spend hours in preparation and still more in thanksgiving. This needs no explanation, for who could explain "the depth of the riches of

the wisdom and knowledge of God"? "How incomprehensible
are his judgments!" cried St. Paul, "And how unsearchable his
ways, for who has known the mind of the Lord?"

—MTR, 185

How tenderly Jesus speaks when he gives himself to his own in
Holy Communion. "My flesh is meat indeed and my blood is
drink indeed. He that eats my flesh and drinks my blood abides
in me and I in him." Oh, what could my Jesus do more than
give me his flesh for my food? No, not even God could do more
nor show a greater love for me.   —MTR, 181

Truly, the tenderness of God's love is most extraordinary. When
we look at the cross, we know how much Jesus loved us then.
When we look at the tabernacle, we know how much he loves
us now. That's why you should ask your parish priests to give
you the joy of having adoration of the Blessed Sacrament at
least once a week.

Be alone with Jesus.

Then your hearts will feel the joy that only he can give.

—MTR, 189

If we really understand the Eucharist, if we really center our
lives on Jesus' body and blood, if we nourish our lives with the
bread of the Eucharist, it will be easy for us to see Christ in that
hungry one next door, the one lying in the gutter, that alcoholic
man we shun, our husband or our wife, or our restless child.
For in them, we will recognize the distressing disguises of the
poor: Jesus in our midst.   —MTR, 231–32

WHAT IS POVERTY?

The sisters are to live by begging. We depend fully on the charity of others. We must not be ashamed to beg from door to

door, if need be. The Lord has promised a reward even for a glass of water given in his name. We become beggars for his sake.

The Lord sometimes suffered real indigence, as can be understood from the multiplication of bread and fish and the picking of grain at the edge of the path. This thought should serve as a comfort to us when our food is scarce.

On the cross Christ was deprived of everything. The cross itself had been given him by Pilate; the nails and the crown, by the soldiers. He was naked.

When he died he was stripped of the cross, the nails, and the crown. He was wrapped in a piece of canvas donated by a charitable soul, and he was buried in a tomb that did not belong to him.

Despite all that, Jesus could have died like a king and could even have been spared death. He chose poverty because he knew that it was the genuine means to possess God and to bring his love to the earth. —HJ, 129–30

We must never get into the habit of being preoccupied with the future. There is no reason to do so. God is there. Once the longing for money comes, the longing also comes for what money can give: superfluities, nice rooms, luxuries at table, more clothes, fans, etc. Our needs will increase, for one thing brings another and the result will be endless dissatisfaction.

Poverty makes us free. That is why we can joke and smile and keep a happy heart for Jesus.

The first true poverty was when "Christ emptied himself." For nine months he was lost in the little space of Mary's bosom: not even St. Joseph knew who he was. Having all things, yet possessing nothing. His birth was also like one of the poorest of the poor. Even our poor have someone to assist them . . . Mary did not. At Nazareth even his people despised him. It was not necessary for Jesus to practice this absolute poverty. There is only one reason: because he desired it. He wanted to be to the fullest "one" of us.   —TS, 56–57

Poverty is necessary because we are working with the poor. When they complain about the food, we can say: we eat the same. They say, "It was so hot last night, we could not sleep." We can reply, "We also felt very hot." The poor have to wash for themselves, go barefoot; we do the same. We have to go down and lift them up. It opens the heart of the poor when we can say we live the same way they do. Sometimes they only have one bucket of water. It is the same with us. The poor have to stand in line; we do too. Food, clothing, everything must be like that of the poor. We have no fasting. Our fasting is to eat the food as we get it.   —TS, 57

Christ being rich emptied himself. This is where contradiction lies. If I want to be poor like Christ — who became poor even though he was rich — I must do the same. Nowadays people want to be poor and live with the poor, but they want to be free to dispose of things as they wish. To have this freedom is to be rich. They want both and they cannot have both. This is another kind of contradiction.

Our poverty is our freedom. This is our poverty — the giving up of our freedom to dispose of things, to choose, to possess. The moment I use and dispose of things as mine, that moment I cease to be poor.

We must strive to acquire the true spirit of poverty which manifests itself in a love for the practice of the virtue of poverty in imitation of Christ — in imitation of him who chose it as the companion of his life on earth when he came to live among us. Christ did not have to lead a life of poverty. Thus he taught us how important it is for our sanctification.   —TS, 56–57

I personally am not worthy of it [the Nobel Peace Prize]. I shall accept it in the name of the poor, because I think that the Committee, in awarding the prize to me, has wished to recognize the existence of the poor in the world.... But what is this? Only a drop compared with the ocean of suffering in this world.

—MTLW, 129

We have received from the poor much more than we have given them. We can learn from the poor how to accept a difficult situation of adversity, to be content with few material goods, to appreciate very much the little that we have.   —MTLL, 51

It would be a shame for us to be wealthier than Jesus. For love of us he subjected himself to poverty. For this reason, our only wealth is Jesus, his love and his presence in our midst....

How can we understand the poor if we ourselves do not live poverty? We are poor for the love of Christ; they are constrained by others to be poor. Poverty frees us from things, from everything and everyone in order to belong completely to Jesus....

My congregation must remain faithful to the poor Jesus. We must live with trust in providence. Our greatest danger is to become rich.... When my congregation becomes wealthy, it will die, because we are not simply social workers. The vow of poverty is a great aid in observing chastity and obedience. By our poverty we choose only Jesus; by obedience we listen to him; by chastity we love him.   —MTLL, 52–53

I see Jesus in every person, and especially in the poor and suffering. The poor do not need our help and assistance.... They have so little, nothing, but they give so much, everything.... Peace will come to the world through the poor because they suffer so much.... The poor are our prayer. They carry God within themselves. Jesus said on the cross: "I thirst." It was not a thirst for water but for love. The goal we seek is to placate this thirst.... Many people who have much are thirsting for love; they want to be understood and recognized as our brothers and sisters. . . . We want to be totally dependent on the charity of others. We should not be ashamed to go from door to door and beg if it is necessary. . . . At times the Lord suffered real poverty. . . . On the cross he was stripped of everything. The cross itself was given by Pilate. The nails and the crown of thorns were given by the soldiers. He was naked. . . . He was wrapped in a sheet donated by a compassionate bystander and was buried in a tomb that was not his. . . . He chose poverty because he knew that this was the authentic means for possessing God and for bringing God's love down to earth. . . . I believe that people attached to riches, who are preoccupied with wealth, are in reality very poor.

But if they put their money at the service of others, they are rich, very rich. . . . We love and help all the poor, both materially and spiritually, because only in this way can we be faithful to Jesus, loving and helping our neighbor. . . . The poor are marvelous people. They have their dignity, as we can readily verify. . . . For us poverty is love before it is renunciation. To love it is necessary to give. To give it is necessary to be free of selfishness. . . . The heart of the poor opens to us when we can show that we live with them. We must humble ourselves in order to lift them up.   — MTLL, 53

We would not be able to understand and effectively help those who lack all, if we did not live like them. All gestures of love, however small they be, in favor of the poor and the unwanted, are important to Jesus.   — GG, 34

We do not accept anything, neither church maintenance, nor salary, nor anything for the work we do, all over the world. Every Missionary of Charity is the poorest of the poor. That is why we can do anything. Whatever is given to the poor is the same for us. We wear the kind of clothes they wear. But ours is a choice. We choose that way. To be able to understand the poor, we must know what is poverty. Otherwise we will speak another language, no? We won't be able to come close to that mother who is anxious for her child. We completely depend on providence. We are like the trees, like the flowers. But we are more important to him than the flowers of the grass. He takes care of them, he takes much greater care of us. That is the beautiful part of the congregation.   —MTB, 217

Our life of poverty is as necessary as the work itself. Only in heaven will we see how much we owe to the poor for helping us to love God better because of them.   —GG, 35

There are people who can afford the luxury to live in great comfort; it is possible that they have earned the privilege by their efforts.

What irritates me is to see that extravagance exists.

It irritates me to see some people waste and throw away things that we could use.   —OW, 80

There are many kinds of poverty. Even in countries where the economic situation seems to be a good one, there are expressions of poverty hidden in a deep place, such as the tremendous loneliness of people who have been abandoned and who are suffering. . . .

As far as I am concerned, the greatest suffering is to feel alone, unwanted, unloved.

The greatest suffering is also having no one, forgetting what an intimate, truly human relationship is, not knowing what it means to be loved, not having a family or friends. . . .

It's we who, with our exclusion and rejecting, push our brothers and sisters to find refuge in alcohol and become drunks. They drink to forget the deprivation of their lives.

          —OW, 91

For us, poverty is freedom. It's total freedom. None of the things we have as Missionaries of Charity we have as property, but we have them as things we use.

The sari that we wear is not ours. We have it to use. The sandals that we wear on our feet are not ours. We have them to use.

Poverty is our strength and a source of happiness.

I want to talk here about the marvelous example of a young lady from a well-to-do family who wrote to me: "For several years Jesus has been inviting me to become a religious. I have tried to discover where he wants me to go. I have gone to several places, but I have found that they had what I have. If I had entered their congregations, I would not have had to give anything up."

It is very clear: the young lady wanted to give everything up.

She wanted to feel free in order to better serve Jesus in the poor.   — OW, 106

One of the expressions of our poverty consists in sewing, the best we can, our own dresses when we discover a tear in them. To walk down the street or around the house wearing a torn sari is by no means a sign of the virtue of poverty.

I usually tell the sisters, "We do not vow the poverty of the beggars, but the poverty of Christ." On the other hand, we should not forget that our bodies are temples of the Holy Spirit. For that reason we should respect them and wear dresses that have been repaired with dignity.   — OW, 108

What is poverty? Poverty is freedom. It is a freedom so that what I possess doesn't own me, so that what I possess doesn't hold me down, so that my possessions don't keep me from sharing or giving of myself. This is the reason why many times I have told nuns, and even priests, who are in charge of educating the children of the wealthy: don't make the mistake of serving the riches of those children instead of the children for whom

Jesus died. You must offer your love to him. Whatever you do at your school or at your university, you can do it for Jesus, just as we do it for Jesus in the slums of the poorest of the poor.

— OHFL, 53

You must continue helping the sisters. I have just told the sisters that we must help our people when they come to us wanting to live a normal human life. We must give them the things they will need when they leave us. We do not need extraordinary things, but only what's necessary so that they may have a joyful life.

As we try to do this for our people, you must protect the poverty of the sisters. We have chosen to be poor. That doesn't mean that we cannot have material goods. In and of itself, it isn't bad to have things, but we have *chosen* not to have them. So you must help to protect us. For once the sisters abound with material goods, we will not have time to tenderly and lovingly care for the poorest of the poor. We will then be too busy caring for things instead of people. So we must continue to have as little as possible. That way Jesus can always come and live comfortably among us.   — OHFL, 100

Spiritual life is union with Jesus — the divine and the human in mutual giving. The only thing Jesus asks is that I commit myself to him, in total poverty, in total forgetfulness of self.

— MTR, 94

Our Lord gives us a living example: From the very first day of his human existence he was brought up in a poverty which no human being will ever be able to experience, because "being rich he made himself poor." As I am his co-worker, his "alter Christus," I must be brought up and nourished by that poverty which our Lord asks of me.   — MTR, 210

You must experience the joy of poverty. Poverty is not only renunciation. Poverty is joy. Poverty is love. My reason for doing

without is that I love Jesus. Unless you experience for yourself
this joy of poverty, you will never understand what I am saying.
                                                              —MTR, 219

THE ART OF HAPPINESS

Joy must be one of the pivots of our life. It is the token of a
generous personality. Sometimes it is also a mantle that clothes
a life of sacrifice and self-giving.

A person who has this gift often reaches high summits. He or
she is like a sun in a community. Let those who suffer find in us
comforting angels.

Why has the work in the slums been blessed by God? Certainly not because of given personal qualities, but because of
the joy that the sisters spread as they pass by.

The people of the world lack our joy. Those who live in the
slums have still less of it. Our joy is the best means to preach
Christianity to the heathen.   —HJ, 127

Joy is one of the most essential things in our society. A Missionary of Charity must be a Missionary of Charity of joy. She must
radiate that joy to everyone. By this sign the world will know
you are Missionaries of Charity. Everyone in the world sees you
and remarks and speaks out about the Missionaries of Charity,
not because of what they do but because they are happy to do
the work they do and live the life they live. "That my joy may
be in you," says Jesus. What is this joy of Jesus? It is the result
of his continual union with God, doing the will of the Father.
This joy is the fruit of union with God, of being in the presence
of God. Living in the presence of God fills us with joy. God is
joy. To bring joy to us, Jesus became man. Mary was the first
one to receive Jesus: "My spirit rejoices in God my Savior." The
child in Elizabeth's womb leapt with joy because Mary carried
Jesus to him.

In Bethlehem, joy filled everyone: the shepherds, the angels, the three kings, Joseph, and Mary. Joy was also the characteristic mark of the first Christians. During the persecution, people used to look for those who had this joy radiating on their faces. By that joy, they knew who the Christians were and thus they persecuted them. St. Paul, whom we are trying to imitate in our zeal, was an apostle of joy. He urged the early Christians to rejoice in the Lord always. Paul's whole life can be summed up in one sentence, "I belong to Christ." Nothing can separate me from the Love of Christ, neither suffering nor persecution nor anything. "I live, now it is no longer I who live but it is Christ who lives in me." That is why St. Paul was so full of joy.

Joy is love, the normal result of a heart burning with love. Our lamp will be burning with sacrifices made out of love if we have joy. Then the Bridegroom will say, "come and possess the kingdom prepared for you." It is a joyful sister who gives most. Everyone loves the one who gives with joy and so does God. Don't we always turn to someone who will give happily and without grumbling? "Joy is a net of love by which we catch souls." Because we are full of joy, everyone wants to be with us and to receive the light of Christ that we possess. A sister filled with joy preaches without preaching. Daily, we pray, "Help me to spread your fragrance," yours, Lord, not mine. Do we realize its meaning? Do we realize our mission of spreading this joy, of radiating this joy daily as we go about our lives?

—TS, 44–46

Joy is not simply a matter of temperament. In the service of God and souls, it is always hard to be joyful — all the more reason why we should try to acquire it and make it grow in our hearts.

Joy is prayer; joy is strength; joy is love; joy is a net of love by which we catch souls. God loves a cheerful giver. She gives most who gives with joy. If in the work you have difficulties and you accept them with joy, with a big smile — in this like in any other thing — they will see your good works and glorify the Father.

The best way to show your gratitude is to accept everything with joy. A joyful heart is the normal result of a heart burning with love.

Joy is a need and a power for us, even physically. A sister who has cultivated a spirit of joy feels less tired and is always ready to go on doing good. Joy is one of the best safeguards against temptations. The devil is a carrier of dust and dirt — he uses every chance to throw what he has at us. A joyful heart knows how to protect itself from such dirt: Jesus can take full possession of our soul only if it surrenders itself joyfully. St. Teresa was worried about her sisters only when she saw any of them lose their joy. God is joy. He is love. A sister filled with joy preaches without preaching. A joyful sister is like the sunshine of God's love, the hope of eternal happiness, the flame of burning love.

In our society, a cheerful disposition is one of the main virtues required for a Missionary of Charity. The spirit of our society is total surrender, loving trust, and cheerfulness. That is why the society expects us to accept humiliations readily and with joy; to live the life of poverty with cheerful trust; to imitate the chastity of Mary, the cause of our joy; to offer cheerful obedience from inward joy; to minister to Christ in his distressing disguise with cheerful devotion.   —TS, 46–47

Cheerfulness should be one of the main points of our religious life. A cheerful giver is a great giver. Cheerfulness is a sign of a generous and mortified person, who, forgetting all things, even herself, tries to please God in all she does for souls. Cheerfulness is often a cloak which hides a life of sacrifice, continual union with God, fervor, and generosity.   —TS, 44

Remember that the passion of Christ always ends in the joy of the resurrection. When you feel in your heart the suffering of Christ, remember that the resurrection will follow, that the joy of Easter will spring forth. Never let yourself be so overcome with sorrow that you forget the joy of the risen Christ.

—MTLL, 60

May the joy of the risen Christ be with you.... Easter is the greatest feast in our congregation.... It gives witness to the new life in Christ that has been given us. —MTLL, 61

Joy is a necessity, a great gift for others and also for ourselves. It is the flame of an ardent love. Joy is prayer; joy is power; joy is love in action. —MTLL, 75

The world today is hungering for the joy that comes from a pure heart, because the pure of heart see God.... A smile costs little but it does so much good.... Joy shines forth in the eyes and in the glance, in one's conversation and in the expression of one's countenance. When people see the happiness in your eyes, they will discover God within you. —MTLL, 77

Ask the Holy Spirit to make you sinners without sin.... We should bear witness to the change, to conversion, with joy. Joy is a fruit of the Holy Spirit, a sign that he dwells within us. Jesus bestowed joy on his disciples: "All this I tell you that my joy may be yours and your joy may be complete" (John 15:11). Our joy is the fruit of generosity, the absence of egoism, of close union with God. God bestows on us the greatest gift — the Holy Spirit — after having given us Jesus. And we are called to give ourselves freely to God and to neighbor with generosity and joy.

—MTLL, 96

The surest means for preaching Christianity to the pagans is our joy, our happiness. Here is one example from my own life. Once a man entered Kalighat. I was there too. After a while he turned to me and said: "I came here with great hatred in my heart for God and for people. I came here empty, without faith, embittered; but when I saw a sister giving careful attention to a patient, and she did it with joy, I realized that God still loves. I am changed. I believe that God exists and he still loves."

—MTLL, 111

A joyful heart is the normal result of a heart burning with love. Joy is not simply a matter of temperament, it is always hard to remain joyful — all the more reason why we should try to acquire it and make it grow in our hearts.

Joy is prayer; joy is strength; joy is love. She gives most who gives with joy.

To children and to the poor, to all those who suffer and are lonely, give them always a happy smile; give them not only your care but also your heart. We may not be able to give much, but we can always give the joy that springs from a heart that is filled with love.

If in your work you have difficulties and you accept them with joy, with a big smile, in this, like many other things, you will see your good works. And the best way to show your gratitude is to accept everything with joy....

If you are joyful, it will shine in your eyes and in your look, in your conversation and in your contentment. You will not be able to hide it because joy overflows.

Joy is very contagious. Try, therefore, to be always overflowing with joy wherever you go.

Joy, according to St. Bonaventure, has been given to man so that he can rejoice in God because of the hope of the eternal good and all the benefits he receives from God. Thus he will know how to rejoice at his neighbor's prosperity, how to feel discontent concerning empty things.

Joy must be one of the pivots of our life. It is the token of a generous personality. Sometimes it is also a mantle that clothes a life of sacrifice and self-giving. A person who has this gift often reaches high summits. He or she is like a sun in a community.

We should ask ourselves, "Have I really experienced the joy of loving?" True love is love that causes us pain, that hurts, and yet brings us joy. That is why we must pray and ask for the courage to love....

May God give back to you in love all the love you have given and all the joy and peace you have sown around you, all over the world. —HW, 27–28

We must be able to radiate the joy of Christ, express it in our actions. If our actions are just useful actions that give no joy to the people, our poor people would never be able to rise up to the call which we want them to hear, the call to come closer to God. We want to make them feel that they are loved. If we went to them with a sad face, we would only make them much more depressed. —SBG, 73

The Missionaries of Charity are firmly convinced that each time we offer help to the poor, we really offer help to Christ.

We try to do this with joy because we cannot go to Christ, even under the guise of the poor, with long faces.

I very often tell the sisters to approach the poor with joy, knowing that they have plenty of reasons to be sad. They don't need us to confirm their sadness for them.

We are committed to feed Christ who is hungry, committed to clothe Christ who is naked, committed to take in Christ who has no home — and to do all this with a smile on our face and bursting with joy.

It is very beautiful to see our sisters, many of them still very young, given totally and with such love to the service of Christ's poor. —OW, 109

Let us keep the joy of loving Jesus in our hearts. And let's share that joy with everyone we meet. Passing on joy is something which is very natural. We have no reason for not being joyful, since Christ is with us. Christ is in our hearts. Christ is in the poor we meet. Christ is in the smile we give to others, and he is in the smile we receive from others.   — OHFL, 87

May the joy of the risen Jesus Christ be with you, to bring joy into your very soul. The good God has given himself to us. "Joy," said the angel in Bethlehem. In his life, Jesus wanted to share his joy with his apostles. "That my joy may be in you." Joy was the password of the first Christians. St. Paul — how often he repeats himself: "Rejoice in the Lord always, again I say to you, rejoice." In return for the great grace of baptism, the priest tells the newly baptized, "May you serve the church joyfully."   — JWS, 36

Cheerfulness is indeed the fruit of the Holy Spirit and a clear sign of the kingdom within. Jesus shared his joy with his disciples: "that my joy may be in you and that your joy be full" (John 15:11). Our joy is a work of our generosity, selflessness, and close union with God; for he gives most who gives with joy, and God loves a cheerful giver.   — JWS, 111

Joy is one of the best safeguards against temptation. The devil is a carrier of dust and dirt; he uses every chance to throw what he has at us. A joyful heart knows how to protect itself from such dirt. Jesus can take full possession of our soul only if it surrenders itself joyfully. "A saint who is sad is a sad saint," St. Francis de Sales used to say. St. Teresa was worried about her sisters only when she saw any of them lose their joy.
                                                — JWS, 125

5

A Fulfilled Life

†

Mother Teresa, by living her Gospel as genuinely as a human being can live and by reflecting the light of Christ to everyone around her and around the world, redefined her task and success. Her call wasn't just to be a social worker, but to awaken others into Christ's love and into the duty of becoming holy, no matter what the place, time, or circumstances might be for them. When we allow God to inflame our hearts to love so much, we cannot go wrong. Mother Teresa, by following her call conscientiously, fulfilled her destiny and lived a truly successful, joyful, and fulfilled life.

AWAKENING

The reason I was given the Nobel prize was because of the poor. However, the prize went beyond appearances. In fact, it awakened consciences in favor of the poor all over the world. It became a sort of reminder that the poor are our brothers and sisters and that we have the duty to treat them with love.

—OW, 107

Let us from the beginning try to live the spirit of the Missionaries of Charity, which is one of total surrender to God, loving trust in each other, and cheerfulness with all. If we really accept this spirit, then, for sure, we will be the true co-workers of Christ — the carriers of his love. This spirit must radiate from your own heart to your family, neighbor, town, country, the world. Let us more and more insist on raising funds of love, of kindness, of understanding, of peace. Money will come if we seek first the Kingdom of God; the rest will be given.

— GG, 33–34

As each sister is to become a co-worker of Christ in the slums, each ought to understand what God and the Missionaries of Charity expect from her. Let Christ radiate and live his life in her and through her in the slums. Let the poor, seeing her, be drawn to Christ and invite him to enter their homes and their lives. Let the sick and suffering find in her a real angel of comfort and consolation. Let the little ones of the streets cling to her because she reminds them of him, the friend of the little ones.

— GG, 34–35

Let there be no pride or vanity in the work. The work is God's work, the poor are God's poor. Put yourself completely under the influence of Jesus, so that he may think his thoughts in your mind, do his work through your hands, for you will be all-powerful with him to strengthen you.   — GG, 36–37

Keep giving Jesus to your people, not by words, but by your example, by your being in love with Jesus, by radiating his holiness and spreading his fragrance of love everywhere you go. Just keep the joy of Jesus as your strength. Be happy and at peace. Accept whatever he gives — and give whatever he takes with a big smile. You belong to him. Tell him: "I am yours, and if you cut me to pieces, every single piece will be only all yours." Let Jesus be the victim and the priest in you.   — GG, 38–39

Let us try more and more to make every sister, brother, and co-worker grow into the likeness of Christ, to allow him to live his life of compassion and humanity in the world of today. Your love for Christ must be great. Keep the light of Christ always burning in your heart, for he alone is the Way to walk. He is the Life to live. He is the Love to love.   —GG, 41

Publicity I don't need. No, no, I do not need it. God's work has to be done in his own way; and he has his own ways and means of making our work known. See what has happened throughout the world and how the sisters have been accepted in places where nobody ever knew anything about them. They have been accepted where many other people find it difficult to live or to be. So I think this is God himself proving that it is his work.
                                                        —GG, 43

There should be less talk; a preaching point is not a meeting point. What do you do then? Take a broom and clean someone's house. That says enough.

All of us are but his instruments, who do our little bit and pass by.   —GG, 44–45

We need money, medicines, clothing, and a thousand other things for the poor we serve. If so many people weren't generous, thousands would be left unaided. Because we still have many poor, needy children and families that live in the streets— not only in Calcutta but in London, Rotterdam, Madrid, Marseilles, and Rome — the need is great. In the last city I mentioned, we have many needy. The sisters go out at night into the streets, especially around the train station, between 10 P.M. and 2 A.M. to pick up the homeless and take them to the home we have on San Gregorio al Cielo.

The last time that I was in Rome, I found it unbearable to see so many homeless people living that way. So I went to see the mayor of Rome and said, "Give me a place for these people, be-

cause they refuse to come with us and would rather stay where
they are." He and his staff responded wonderfully. In a few days
they offered us a very nice place near the Termini Train Station.
At present, all those who have nowhere else to spend the night
except in the streets go there and sleep in beds. In the morning
they leave.

This is the wonderful part of our vocation, that as Missionaries of Charity we have created an awareness of the poor in
the whole world. Twenty years ago no one would have believed
that there were hungry, naked men and women around. Today
the whole world knows our poor because of our work. And
they want to share.

Why is our congregation known all over the world today? It
is because people see what we do: feeding the hungry, clothing
the naked, taking care of the sick and the dying. Because they
see, they believe.   —HW, 40–42

Sacrifice is at the heart of Christian faith. The people of God
in Old Testament times offered animals for their sins — lambs,
goats, bulls, and pigeons. Jesus offered himself as a perfect,
final sacrifice so that the animal sacrifices would not have to
be repeated.

Sacrifice, surrender, and suffering are not popular topics
nowadays. Our culture makes us believe that we can have it
all, that we should demand our rights, that with the right tech-
nology all pain and problems can be overcome. This is not my
attitude toward sacrifice. I know that it is impossible to re-
lieve the world's suffering unless God's people are willing to
surrender to God, to make sacrifices, and to suffer along with
the poor.

From the beginning of time the human heart has felt the need
to offer God a sacrifice. What is an acceptable sacrifice? One
that is good for the people of God. One that is made on behalf
of the world.   —HW, 47–48

Some of my sisters work in Australia. On a reservation, among the Aborigines, there was an elderly man. I can assure you that you have never seen a situation as difficult as that poor old man's. He was completely ignored by everyone. His home was disordered and dirty.

I told him, "Please, let me clean your house, wash your clothes, and make your bed." He answered, "I'm okay like this. Let it be."

I said again, "You will be still better if you allow me to do it."

He finally agreed. So I was able to clean his house and wash his clothes. I discovered a beautiful lamp, covered with dust. Only God knows how many years had passed since he last lit it.

I said to him, "Don't you light your lamp? Don't you ever use it?"

He answered, "No. No one comes to see me. I have no need to light it. Who would I light it for?"

I asked, "Would you light it every night if the sisters came?"

He replied, "Of course."

From that day on the sisters committed themselves to visiting him every evening. We cleaned the lamp, and the sisters would light it every evening.

Two years passed. I had completely forgotten that man. He sent this message: "Tell my friend that the light she lit in my life continues to shine still."

I thought it was a very small thing. We often neglect small things.   —HW, 53–54

One year I wanted to do something special for our sisters. I sent out a newsletter to each one of them, to each community, suggesting that each one write down what she thought was beautiful in her sisters and her community. I asked that each sister send her answer to me.

A thousand letters arrived. Just imagine! I had to sit down

and read each one, making a list of each community and all the sisters. Later I returned the letters to the communities.

The sisters were surprised that someone would notice such beautiful things in them — that there was someone who was able to see them. All of this fostered a beautiful spirit of love, understanding, and sharing.

I feel that we too often focus on the negative aspects of life, on what is bad. If we were more willing to see the good and the beautiful things that surround us, we would be able to transform our families. From there, we would change our next-door neighbors and then others who live in our neighborhood or city. We would be able to bring peace and love to our world, which hungers so much for these things.   —HW, 59–60

One day, we picked up a man off the street who looked like a fairly well-to-do person. He was completely drunk. He couldn't even stand up because he was so drunk!

We took him to our home. The sisters treated him with love, care, and kindness.

After a fortnight, he told the sisters, "Sisters, my heart is open. Through you I have come to realize that God loves me. I've felt his tender love for me. I want to go home." And we helped him get ready to go home.

After a month, he came back to our home and gave the sisters his first paycheck. He told the sisters, "Do to others what you have done to me." And he walked away a different person.

Love had brought him back to his family, to his children's tenderness, to his wife's understanding love.

Let us ask Our Lady to teach us how to love and how to have the courage to share.   —HW, 61–62

One evening we went out and rescued four people off the streets. One of them was in a desperate condition. I told the sisters, "You take care of the others. I will care for this one who is worse off." I did everything for her that my love could do. I put her into bed, and I saw a beautiful smile light up her face. She squeezed my hand and only managed to say two words: "Thank you." And then she closed her eyes.

I couldn't help but ask myself there beside her body, "What would I have said if I had been in her place?" My answer was very simple. I would have said that I was hungry, that I was dying, that I was cold. Or I would have said that this or that part of my body hurt or something like that. But she gave me much more. She gave me her grateful love. And she died with a smile on her face.

Just like that man we rescued from among the debris in the gutter, the one who was half-eaten by worms, this woman responded in grateful love. That man told us, "I have lived like an animal in the street, but I am going to die like an angel surrounded by love and care." It was marvelous to witness the greatness of a man who could talk like that, who could die that way without cursing anyone, without lashing out at anyone, without drawing any comparisons. He died like an angel.

—HW, 63–64

One day an Australian man came and made a substantial donation. But as he did this he said, "This is something external. Now I want to give something of myself." He now comes regularly to the house of the dying to shave the sick men and to converse with them. This man gives not only his money but also his time. He could have spent it on himself, but what he wants is to give of himself.

I often ask for gifts that have nothing to do with money. There are so many other things one can give. What I desire is the presence of the donor, for him to touch those to whom he gives, to smile at them, for him to pay attention to them. All of this is very meaningful for those people.

I urge people to join our work, for our profit and for the profit of everyone. I never ask them for money or any material things. I ask them to bring their love, to offer the sacrifice of their hands. When these people run across those in need, their first move is to do something. When they come the second time, they already feel committed. After some time they feel they belong to the poor and they are filled with the need to love. They discover who they are and what it is that they themselves can give.

I think that a person who is attached to riches, who lives with the worry of riches, is actually very poor. If this person puts his money at the service of others, then he is rich, very rich.

—HW, 69–70

I will tell you another good example of how generous and great people are.

We had picked up a young orphan boy whose mother had died in the home for dying destitutes. She had come from a good family, but had come down in life because of difficult circumstances.

The boy grew up and wanted to become a priest. When he was asked, "Why do you want to become a priest?" he gave a very simple answer. "I want to do for other children what Mother Teresa has done for me. I want to love as she loved me. I want to serve as she served me."

Today he is a priest, devoted to loving all those who have nothing and no one — those who have forgotten what human love is, or the warmth of a human touch, or even the kindness of a smile.   —HW, 81–82

Don't search for Jesus in far lands — he is not there. He is close to you; he is with you. Just keep the lamp burning and you will always see him. Keep on filling the lamp with all these little drops of love, and you will see how sweet is the Lord you love.

The fullness of our heart is expressed in our eyes, in our touch, in what we write, in what we say, in the way we walk, the way we receive, the way we serve. That is the fullness of our heart expressing itself in many different ways.

I wish to live in this world, which is so far from God, which
has turned so much from the light of Jesus, to help them —
our poor, to take upon me something of their sufferings. For
only by being one with them can we redeem them, that is, by
bringing God into their lives and bringing them to God. Even
God cannot force himself on anyone who does not want him.
Faith is a gift.   —HW, 90–91

IN PURSUIT OF HOLINESS

Holiness is the main reason for the existence of our society.
For us, holiness should not be difficult — for in giving wholehearted free service to the poorest of the poor, we are with Jesus
twenty-four hours. And, since every Missionary of Charity is
the poorest of the poor, we live and observe the fourth vow
even when we do small things for each other.

Nothing can make me holy except the presence of God, and
to me the presence of God is fidelity to small things. Fidelity to
small things will lead you to Christ. Infidelity to small things
will lead you to sin.   —TS, 32–33

All of us have one Father, the heavenly Father, and one Mother,
Our Lady. Religious are at the very heart of our holy Mother
Church; they are servants of the Lord, as the Virgin Mary was.
... The unique source of unity and holiness is Jesus in the Eucharist.... By nourishing ourselves on his body and blood, we
shall become one body with Jesus and through Jesus, thanks
to his great love.... Holiness is not the privilege of a few; it is
a duty for every Christian, for me and for you. Our work is
a marvelous means for our sanctification.... With holiness you
will be able to love and serve others in your and my city of
Skopje....

This is the holiness of everyday life: to live in peace and in
love with God and our neighbor, to help all those who have

need of our hands, our words, our smile, our heart; to be always ready for sacrifice, for service, for love. That is a very simple but a profound and authentic holiness. Only holiness can make us capable of perfect sacrifice, of total giving. What is a saint? A resolute soul; a soul that makes use of its power for action. Paul did not intend to say anything else when he affirmed: "I can do all things in him who strengthens me."   —MTLL, 103

Holiness is not a privilege of the few; it is the duty of all believers, and especially of us consecrated persons.

—MTLL, 131

Make sure that you let God's grace work in your souls by accepting whatever he gives you, and giving him whatever he takes from you. True holiness consists in doing God's will with a smile.   —GG, 37

Thoughtfulness is the beginning of great sanctity. If you learn this art of being thoughtful, you will become more and more Christlike, for his heart was meek and he always thought of others. Jesus "went about doing good." Our Lady did nothing else in Cana but thought of the need of the others and made their need known to Jesus. The thoughtfulness of Jesus and Mary and Joseph was so great that it made Nazareth the abode of God Most High. If we also have that kind of thoughtfulness for each other, our communities will really become the abode of God Most High.   —JWS, 101–2

The special aim of the society is to labor at the conversion and sanctification of the poor in the slums; that is, by nursing the sick and the dying, by gathering and teaching little street children, by visiting and caring for beggars and their children, by giving shelter to the abandoned.

    To labor at the conversion and sanctification of the poor in the slums involves hard, ceaseless toiling, without results, with-

out counting the cost.... To convert and sanctify is the work
of God, but God has chosen the Missionaries of Charity in
his great mercy to help him in his own work. It is a special
grace granted to the Missionaries of Charity, without any merit
of theirs, to carry the light of Christ into the dark holes of
the slums.

"I have other food to eat that you know not of. Lift up your
eyes and see the fields, white and ready for the harvest" (John
4:32–35). This is my food, the conversion and sanctification
of souls.   —TS, 139–40

One of the doorways to holiness is obedience. To be able to
obey, we must be free. That is why we take a vow of poverty,
having nothing. Jesus came down and was subject. We must go
down in the depths of our hearts and see how to bring holiness
into our society.   —TS, 78

Our progress in holiness depends on God and ourselves — on
God's grace and on our will to be holy. We must have a real
living determination to reach holiness. "I will be a saint" means
I will despoil myself of all that is not God; I will strip my heart
of all created things; I will live in poverty and detachment; I will
renounce my will, my inclinations, my whims and fancies, and
make myself a willing slave to the will of God.   —SBG, 48

In order to be saints, you have to seriously want to be one.

St. Thomas Aquinas assures us that holiness "is nothing else
but a resolution made, the heroic act of a soul that surrenders
to God." And he adds: "Spontaneously we love God, we run
towards him, we get close to him, we possess him."

Our willingness is important because it changes us into the
image of God and likens us to him! The decision to be holy is
a very dear one.

Renunciation, temptations, struggles, persecutions, and all

kinds of sacrifices are what surround the soul that has opted
for holiness.   —OW, 3

If we do the work for God and for his glory, we may be
sanctified.   —OW, 3

The president of Mexico sent for me. I told him that he had to
become holy as a president: not a Missionary of Charity, but as
a president.

He looked at me a bit surprised, but it is like that: we have
to become holy, each of us, in the place where God has put us.
                                                             —MLP, 83

I recently went to a meeting of the Calcutta co-workers. I told
them, "Holiness is not a luxury; you are all invited to it."

I said this to Hindus, Moslems, Jains, Parsees, Christians.

They seemed pleased to hear it. I developed the theme in this
way. Holiness is to love God and love men. It is therefore not
a luxury reserved for a few favored persons. All are invited to
be holy.   —MLP, 46

The church of God needs saints today. This imposes a great responsibility on us sisters, to fight against our own ego and love
of comfort that leads us to choose a comfortable and insignificant mediocrity. We are called upon to make our lives a rivalry
with Christ; we are called upon to be warriors in a sari, for the
church needs fighters today. Our war cry has to be "Fight—not
flight."   —JWS, 40

The perfect will of God for us: you must be holy. Holiness is
the greatest gift that God can give us because for that reason he
created us. For that reason you have become Universal Brothers
of the Word. You have not come here just to spend time, even
to spend your time praying. You have come here to be his love,
his compassion. You have been sent.   —JWS, 73

If we really want to grow in holiness through obedience let us turn constantly to our Lady to teach us how to obey, to Jesus who was obedient unto death: he, being God, "went down and was subject to them." — JWS, 107

Total surrender to God must come in small details just as it comes in big details. It's nothing but that single word, "Yes, I accept whatever you give, and I give whatever you take." And this is just a simple way for us to be holy. We must not create difficulties in our own minds. To be holy doesn't mean to do extraordinary things, to understand big things, but it is a simple acceptance, because I have given myself to God, because I belong to him — my total surrender. He could put me here. He could put me there. He can use me. He cannot use me. It doesn't matter because I belong so totally to him that he can do just what he wants to do with me. — JWS, 27–28

We are but instruments that God deigns to use; these instruments bring forth fruit in the measure that they are united to God, as St. Paul says: "I have planted, Apollos watered, but God gave the increase." We obtain grace in proportion to our sanctity, to our fervor, and to our degree of union with our Lord. Sanctity is the soul of the true apostolate. Therefore, we must apply ourselves heart and soul to the learning of this sanctity. — JWS, 30

We shall always keep in mind that our community is not composed of those who are already saints, but of those who are trying to become saints. Therefore we shall be extremely patient with each other's faults and failures. — MTR, 87

Jesus wants us to be holy as his Father is.

Holiness consists of carrying out God's will with joy.

Each one of us is what he is in the eyes of God. We are all called to be saints. There is nothing extraordinary about this

call. We all have been created in the image of God to love and
to be loved.   —MTR, 146

If we earnestly desire holiness, self-denial must enter our lives
fully after prayer. The easiest form of self-denial is control over
our bodily senses. We must practice interior mortification and
bodily penances also. How generous are we with God in our
mortifications?   —MTR, 147

A day alone with Jesus is apt to spur us on in the vigorous pursuit of holiness through personal love for Jesus. Jesus desires
our perfection with unspeakable ardor. "It is God's will that
you grown in holiness" (1 Thess. 4:3). His Sacred Heart is filled
with an insatiable longing to see us advance toward holiness.
                                                    —MTR, 147

Am I convinced of Christ's love for me and mine for him? This
conviction is like a sunlight which makes the sap of life rise and
the buds of sanctity bloom. This conviction is the rock on which
sanctity is built. What must we do to get this conviction? We
must know Jesus, love Jesus, serve Jesus. We know him through
prayers, meditations, and spiritual duties. We love him through
Holy Mass and the sacraments and through that intimate union
of love.   —MTR, 147

Foresight is the beginning of holiness. If you learn this art of
foreseeing, you will be more and more like Christ, for his heart
was sweet and he would always think about others.
                                                    —MTR, 150

I cannot long for a clear perception of my progress along the
route, nor long to know precisely where I am on the path of
holiness. I ask Jesus to make me a saint. I leave it to him to
choose the means that can lead me in that direction.
                                                    —MTR, 149

To become holy we need humility and prayer. Jesus taught us how to pray, and he also told us to learn from him to be meek and humble of heart. Neither of these can we do unless we know what is silence. Both humility and prayer grow from an ear, mind, and tongue that have lived in silence with God, for in the silence of the heart God speaks.   —MTR, 149

We all know that there is God who loves us, who has made us. We can turn and ask him, "My Father, help me now. I want to be holy, I want to be good, I want to love." Holiness is not a luxury for the few; it is not just for some people. It is meant for you and for me, for all of us. It is a simple duty, because if we learn to love, we learn to be holy.   —MTR, 151

"THE SECRET OF CHRISTIAN SUCCESS"

Lord, help us to see in your crucifixion and resurrection an example of how to endure and seemingly to die in the agony and conflict of daily life, so that we may live more fully and creatively. You accepted patiently and humbly the rebuffs of human life, as well as the tortures of your crucifixion and passion. Help us to accept the pains and conflicts that come to us each day as opportunities to grow as people and become more like you. Enable us to go through them patiently and bravely, trusting that you will support us. Make us realize that it is only by frequent deaths of ourselves and our self-centered desires that we can come to live more fully; for it is only by dying with you that we can rise with you.   —GG, 73–74

Here is the secret of Christian success. Christ gave his life so that it could become our life, present in every individual, in every family.   —MTLL, 62

We should let the good God carry out every project in the future, for yesterday is gone, tomorrow has not yet arrived, and we have only today to make him known, loved, and served.

—MTLL, 63

Often we Christians constitute the worst obstacle for those who try to become closer to Christ; we often preach a Gospel we do not live. This is the principal reason why people of the world don't believe.   —OW, 100

If day after day we devote ourselves to the perfect fulfillment of our spiritual duties, he will gradually admit us to a closer intimacy so that even outside the time dedicated to prayer we shall find no difficulty in remaining conscious of the divine presence. On the other hand, the diligent practice of the presence of God by means of fervent aspirations in our labors and in our recreations will be rewarded with more abundant graces. We must endeavor to live alone with Jesus in the sanctuary of our inmost heart.   —JWS, 35

I fulfill what is wanting in the Passion of Christ. It is very difficult to understand what the connection is between our penances and the Passion of Christ. We must constantly follow in the footsteps of Jesus Christ and in a certain manner crucify our own flesh. Our suffering will never come to that degree reached by the saints and martyrs.   —JWS, 36

The fullness of our heart comes in our actions: how I treat that leper, how I treat that dying person, how I treat the homeless. Sometimes it is more difficult to work with the street people than with the people in our homes for the dying because the dying are peaceful and waiting; they are ready to go to God. You can touch the sick and believe, or you can touch the leper and believe, that it is the body of Christ you are touching, but it is much more difficult when these people are drunk or shouting to think that this is Jesus in that distressing disguise. How clean and loving our hands must be to be able to bring that compassion to them! —JWS, 70

We all long for heaven where God is, but we have it in our power to be in heaven with him right now, to be happy with him this moment. But being happy with him now means loving as he loves, helping as he helps, giving as he gives, serving as he serves, rescuing as he rescues — and being with him twenty-four hours a day. —JWS, 83

Love begins at home, right inside our community. We cannot love outside unless we really love our brothers and sisters inside. So I say we need a very clean heart to be able to see God. When we all see God in each other, we will love one another as he loves us all. That is the fulfillment of the law, to love one another. This is all Jesus came to teach us: that God loves us, and that he wants us to love one another as he loves us.

—JWS, 103

Our contemplation is pure joy in our awareness of the presence of the Lord. It is pure silence in our experience of his fullness. Our contemplation is our life. It is not a matter of doing but being. It is the possession of our spirit by the Holy Spirit breathing into us the plenitude of God and sending us forth to the whole creation as his personal message of love. —JWS, 115

Even Almighty God cannot fill what is already full. We must be empty if we want God to fill us with his fullness. Our Lady had to be empty before she could be full of grace. She had to declare that she was the handmaid of the Lord before God could fill her. So also we must be empty of all pride, all jealousy, of all selfishness before God can fill us with his love.

We must be able to give ourselves so completely to God that he must be able to possess us. We must "give whatever he takes and take whatever he gives."

How unlike him we are. How little love, how little compassion, how little forgiveness, how little kindness we have. We are not worthy to be so close to him — to enter his heart. For his heart is still open to embrace us. His head is still crowned with thorns, his hands nailed to the cross today.

Let us find out: "Are the nails mine? That spit on his face, is it mine? What part of his body, of his mind, has suffered because of me?" We should ask, not with anxiety or fear, but with a meek and humble heart. Let us find out what part of his body has wounds inflicted by our sin. Let us not go alone but put our hands in his. He has called us in a special way, given us a name. We belong to him with all our misery, our sin, our weakness, our goodness. We are his.   —MTR, 181–82

You brothers who in a special way have taken the word of God, how clean your heart must be to be able to speak from the fullness of your heart! But before you speak, it is necessary for you to listen, for God speaks in the silence of the heart. You have to listen, and only then, from the fullness of your heart, you speak and God listens.   —JWS, 72

You may be writing, and the fullness of your heart will come to your hand also. Your heart may speak through writing. Your heart may speak through your eyes also. You know that when you look at people they must be able to see God in your eyes. If you get distracted and worldly then they will not be able to see God like that. The fullness of our heart is expressed in our eyes, in our touch, in what we write, in what we say, in the way we walk, the way we receive, the way we need. That is the fullness of our heart expressing itself in many different ways.
                                          —MTR, 95

Pope Paul says that vocation means the capacity to heed the imploring voices of the world of innocent souls of those who suffer, who have no comfort, no guidance, no love. This requirement is beautifully fulfilled by our vow of wholehearted and free service to the poor. Just as Christ went about doing good, healing the sick, casting out devils, preaching the kingdom of God, we too spend ourselves untiringly in seeking, in towns as well as villages, even amid the dustbins, the poor, the abandoned, the sick, the infirm, the dying, and in taking care of them, helping them, visiting them, and giving them the message of Christ, and trying our best to bring them to God.

—MTR, 202

The contemplative and apostolic fruitfulness of our way of life depends on our being rooted in Christ Jesus our Lord by our deliberate choice of small and simple means for the fulfillment of our mission and by our fidelity to humble work of love among the spiritually poorest, identifying ourselves with them, sharing their poverty and insecurities until it hurts.   —MTR, 207

Our brothers and sisters are found scattered around the world. It is wonderful to see how people welcome us, to hear them exclaim, "The sisters and brothers are Christ's love among us." Remember me telling you how the sisters arrived in the Muslim country of Yemen. It was the first time in eight hundred years that a Catholic sister had been seen in that country. The head of the government of that country wrote to a priest in Rome, saying, "The sisters' presence has kindled a new light in the lives of our people." The sisters are not called Missionaries of Charity there. They are called the 'Carriers of God's Love.' "

—MTR, 261

A Missionary of Charity is just a little instrument in the hands of God. We must try to keep it always like that — being just a small instrument in his hands. Very often I feel like a little pencil in God's hand. He does the writing; he does the thinking; he does the movement — I have only to be a pencil and nothing else.

- You are being sent; you have not chosen for yourself where you want to go; and you are *sent* just as Jesus was *sent* to us.

- You are sent not to teach but to learn: learn to be meek and humble of heart. That is just what Jesus has asked us to do: "Learn of me for I am meek and humble of heart."

- You are sent to serve and not to be served: Go to serve with a humble heart. Never escape the hard work. Be always the first one to do it.

- Go to be a cause of joy to your communities.

- Go with zeal and love for the poor.

- Go in haste, like Our Lady, to serve.

- Choose the hardest thing. Go with a humble heart, with a generous heart. Don't go with ideas that don't fit into our way of life: with big, big ideas about theology and what you would like to teach, but rather go to learn and to serve.

- Share what you have received, with a humble heart.

- Go to the poor with great tenderness. Serve the poor with tender, compassionate love.

- Say yes to peace with your tongue. Close your mouth rather than speaking a word which will hurt anyone.

- Go to give yourselves without any reservation. Give yourselves wholeheartedly, unreservedly.

—TS, 126–28

When you look at the inner workings of electrical things, often you see small and big wires, new and old, cheap and expensive lined up. Until the current passes through them there will be no light. That wire is you and me. The current is God. We have the power to let the current pass through us, use us, produce the light of the world — Jesus. Or we can refuse to be used and allow darkness to spread.

Our Lady was the most wonderful wire. She allowed God to fill her to the brim. By her surrender "Be it done to me according to thy word" she became "full of grace." The moment she was filled by this current, by the grace of God, she went in haste to Elizabeth's house to connect the wire, John, to the current, Jesus. As his mother said, "This child, John, leapt up with joy at your voice." Let us ask Our Lady to come into our lives also and make the current, Jesus, use us to go round the world — especially in our own communities so that we can continue connecting the wires of the hearts of men and women with the current, Jesus. —TS, 151–52

God loves me. I'm not here just to fill a place, just to be a number. He has chosen me for a purpose. I know it. He will fulfill it if I don't put an obstacle in his way. He will not force me. God could have forced Our Lady. Jesus could have come just like that. The Holy Spirit could have come. But God wanted Mary to say yes. It is the same with us. God doesn't force us, but he wants us to say yes. —MTR, 194

If something belongs to me, I've got full power to use it as I want. I belong to Jesus; he can do to me whatever he wants. The work is not our vocation. I can do this work without being a religious. Can you tell me why we become Missionaries of Charity? The work is not our vocation. Our vocation is to belong to him. —MTR, 202

We have a great deal of worth in the eyes of God. I never tire of saying over and over again that God loves us. In the Constitution of the Missionaries of Charity, we have a beautiful statement about chastity. It says, "Jesus offers his lifelong, faithful, and personal friendship, embracing us in tenderness and love." It is a wonderful thing that God himself loves me tenderly. That is why we should have courage, joy, and the conviction that nothing can separate us from the love of Christ.

— MTR, 197

Total abandonment consists of giving oneself fully to God because God has given himself to us. If God, who owes us nothing, is willing to give us nothing less than himself, can we respond by giving him only a part of ourselves? Renouncing myself, I give myself to God that he might live in me.

How poor we would be if God had not given us the power to give ourselves over to him! Instead, how rich we are right now!

How easy it is to conquer God! We give ourselves to him, and God becomes ours, and now we have nothing but God. The prize with which God rewards our self-abandonment is himself.

— HJ, 125

The fifteenth chapter of St. John will bring us close to Christ. This chapter of St. John I think is so fitting for us because the branch on the vine is exactly what every co-worker is. The Father, being the gardener, has to prune that branch to be able to bring forth much fruit and the fruit that we have to bring into the world is very beautiful — the love of the Father (as the Father has loved me, so I have loved you). Each one of us is a branch.

When I was last in Rome I wanted to give a little instruction to my novice sisters and I thought that this chapter was the most beautiful means of understanding what we are to Jesus and what Jesus is to us. But I had not realized as those young sisters had realized when they looked at the joining of the vine and the branches that the joining was so tight — as if the vine were afraid that something or somebody would separate the branch from it.

The other thing that the sisters drew my attention to was that when they looked at the vine they could see no fruit. All the fruit was on the branches. Then they told me that the humility of Jesus is so great that he needs the branch to produce the fruit. That is why he has taken so much care over the joining — to be able to produce that fruit he has made it a joining that somebody will have to use force to separate. The Father, the gardener, prunes the branch to bring more fruit and the branch silently, lovingly, unconditionally, lets itself be pruned. We know what the pruning is for in all our lives there must be the cross and the closer we are to him the greater is the touch of the cross, and the pruning is much more intimate and delicate.

Each one of us is a co-worker of Christ, the branch on that vine, so what does it mean for you and me to be a co-worker of Christ? It means to abide in his love, to have his joy, to spread his compassion, to be a witness to his presence in the world.

—LS, 59–60

MODERN SPIRITUAL MASTERS SERIES

Other volumes in this series are available at your local bookstore or directly through Orbis Books. Previously published volumes include:

Dietrich Bonhoeffer

Writings Selected with an Introduction
by Robert Coles

ISBN 1-57075-194-3.

Henri Nouwen

Writings Selected with an Introduction
by Robert A. Jonas

ISBN 1-57075-197-8.

Anthony de Mello

Writings Selected with an Introduction
by William Dych, S.J.

ISBN 1-57075-283-4.

Thomas Merton

Essential Writings
Selected with an Introduction
by Christine Bochen

ISBN 1-57075-331-8.

Pierre Teilhard de Chardin

Writings Selected with an Introduction
by Ursula King

ISBN 1-57075-248-6.

Thich Nhat Hanh

Essential Writings
Edited by Robert Ellsberg
Introduction by Sister Annabel Laity
ISBN 1-57075-370-9.

Please support your local bookstore or
call 1-800-258-5838.
For a free catalog, please write us at

Orbis Books, Box 308
Maryknoll, NY 10545-0308

or visit our website at www.orbisbooks.com

Thank you for reading *Mother Teresa*. We hope you enjoyed it.